Outline Maps of Canada

Grades K-3

About this book:
"Outline Maps of Canada" is an important resource to help introduce and review mapping skills, with an emphasis on Canadian maps. Almost every map included can be used to teach or review the use of: directions on a compass rose, symbols on a Legend and mapping terms such as border, boundary and hemisphere.

The maps will help students:

- Recognize the Shape of Canada
- Locate Canada in North America and the World
- Recognize and locate Canada's provinces, territories and capital cities
- Begin to recognize parallels of latitude and meridians of longitude.
- Use simple scale on maps of Canada
- Provide starting points for inquiry or research on specific provinces and territories
- Use a grid on a map
- Locate and name rivers and large bodies of water

Written by Lynda Golletz, B.A.
Illustrated by S&S Learning Materials

About the author:
Ms. Golletz has 33 years of primary and junior level teaching experience and was the recipient of the "Chairman's Quality Plus Award," presented for outstanding teaching. Ms. Golletz has been recognized by her colleagues for her exemplary teaching skills. She has given many popular educational workshops and has a strong curriculum background. She has authored and coauthored several well-received educational documents. Ms. Golletz has crossed Canada many times by train and automobile. These travels strengthened her love for this country and her knowledge of its geography.

Copyright © S&S Learning Materials 2011

This publication may be reproduced under licence from Access Copyright, or with the express written permission of On The Mark Press / S&S Learning Materials, or as permitted by law.

All rights are otherwise reserved, and no part of this publication may be reproduced, stored in a retrieval system, or transmitted in any form or by any means, electronic, mechanical, photocopying, scanning, recording or otherwise, except as specifically authorized. "We acknowledge the financial support of the Government of Canada through the Book Publishing Industry Development Program (BPIDP) for this project."

All Rights Reserved
Printed in Canada

Published in Canada by:
S&S Learning Materials
15 Dairy Avenue
Napanee, Ontario
K7R 1M4
www.sslearning.com

SSJ1-79 ISBN: 9781554951031

© S&S Learning Materials

 # Outline Maps of Canada

Table of Contents

Teacher Notes 3	Outline Map of Québec 31
Map of the World With Continents and Labels 5	Map of New Brunswick 32
Map of the World with Continents Without Labels 6	Outline Map of New Brunswick 33
Map of North America and Labels 7	Map of Nova Scotia 34
Map of North America Without Labels 8	Outline Map of Nova Scotia 35
Canada on a Globe 9	Map of Prince Edward Island 36
Canada on a Globe 10	Outline Map of Prince Edward Island 37
The Shape of Canada 11	Map of Newfoundland and Labrador 38
The Shape of Canada 12	Outline Map of Newfoundland and Labrador 39
Canada Map Without Political Boundaries 13	Map of Nunavut 40
Canada on a Grid Map 14	Outline Map of Nunavut 41
Canada Map With Provinces and Territories and	Map of Yukon 42
Capital Cities With Labels 15	Outline Map of Yukon 43
Canada Map With Provinces and Territories and	Map of Northwest Territories 44
Capital Cities Without Labels 16	Outline Map of Northwest Territories 45
Colour on the Map of Canada 17	Physical Regions of Canada With Labels 46
Canada's Main Bodies of Water With Labels ...18	Physical Regions of Canada Without Labels 47
Canada's Main Bodies of Water Without Labels 19	Map Showing Parallels of Latitude in Canada 48
	Map Showing Meridians of Longitude in Canada ... 49
Teacher's Note: The following 26 pages will follow this pattern. Each province/territory will be represented by two pages of maps. Map one will have the main cities and rivers with labels. Map two will be a blank outline map.	Using Simple Scale on a Map of Canada 50
	Using Simple Scale on a Map of Canada 51
	Hemispheres 52
	Locating Hemispheres Using a Map With Labels ... 53
	Locating and labelling Hemispheres on a Map 54
Map of British Columbia 20	Cardinal Directions 55
Outline Map of British Columbia 21	Intermediate Directions 56
Map of Alberta 22	Map Showing the Great Lakes With Labels 57
Outline Map of Alberta 23	Outline Map showing The Great Lakes Without Labels . 58
Map of Saskatchewan 24	Map Showing Canada's Larger Lakes With Labels 59
Outline Map of Saskatchewan 25	Map Showing Canada's Larger Lakes Without Labels ... 60
Map of Manitoba 26	Map Showing Some of Canada's Major Rivers 61
Outline Map of Manitoba 27	Canada Map Cards 62
Map of Ontario 28	Answer Key 64
Outline Map of Ontario 29	
Map of Québec 30	

SSJ1-79 ISBN: 9781554951031

Canada in the World

Asia

Australia

Europe

Africa

North America

South America

Antarctica

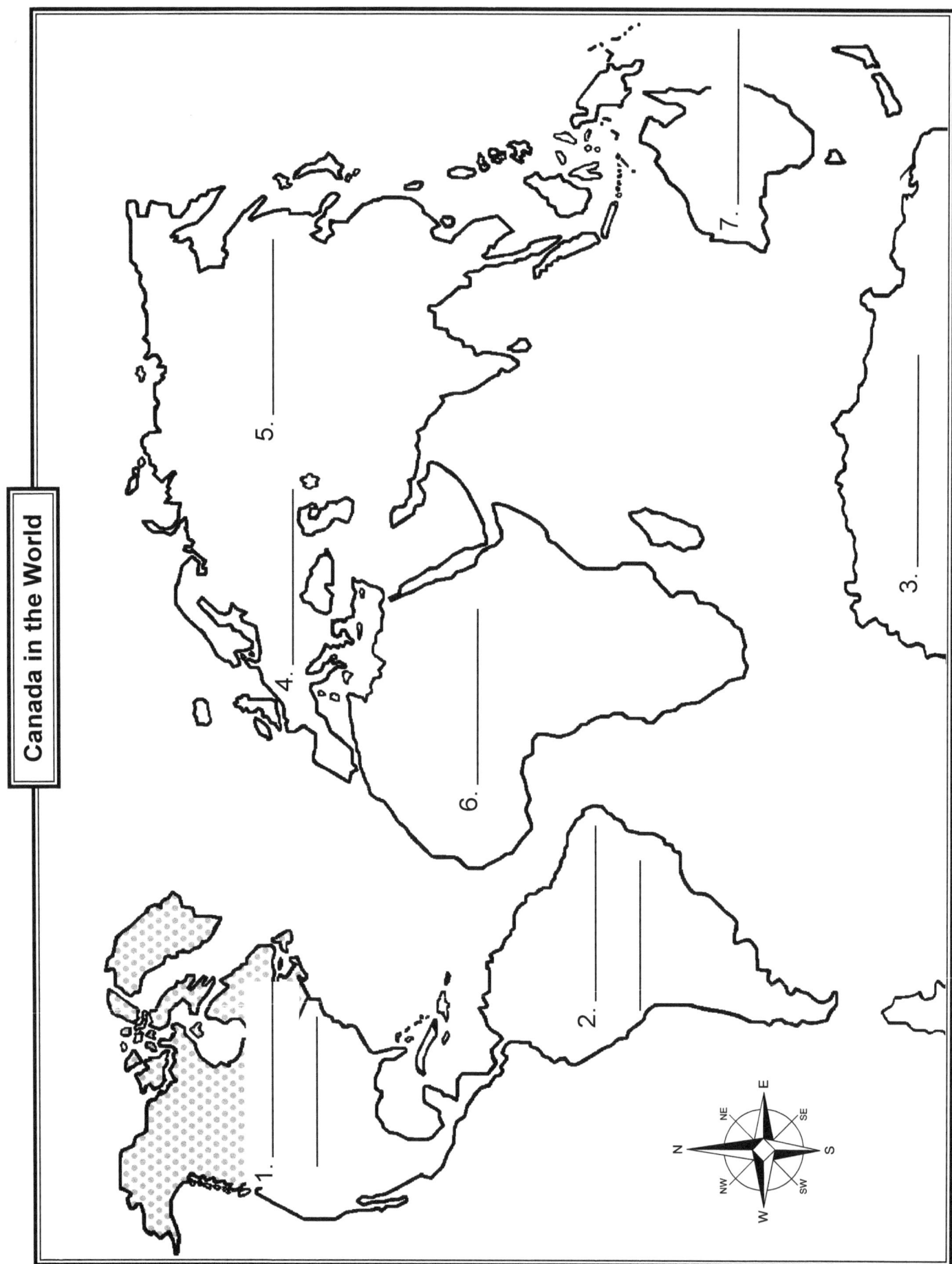

Canada in North America

Canada in North America

Canada on a Globe

Canada on a Globe - Various Views

Colour Canada red on each globe.

Put an X on the globe that does not show Canada.

The Shape of Canada

Trace around the shape of Canada.

Trace the name Canada.

Use a red crayon to lightly colour Canada.

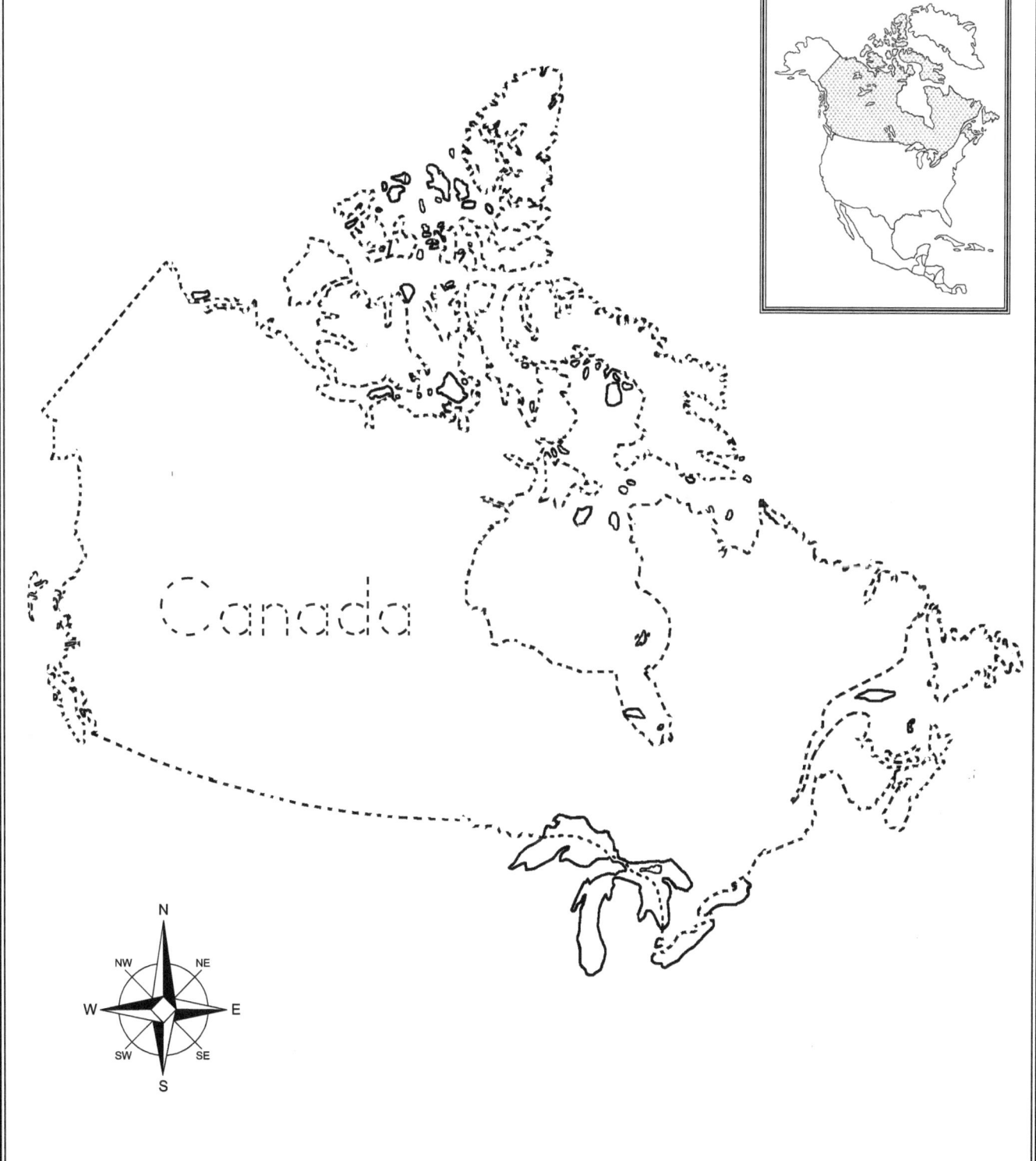

Can You Find Canada?

Draw a big red circle around the maps showing Canada.

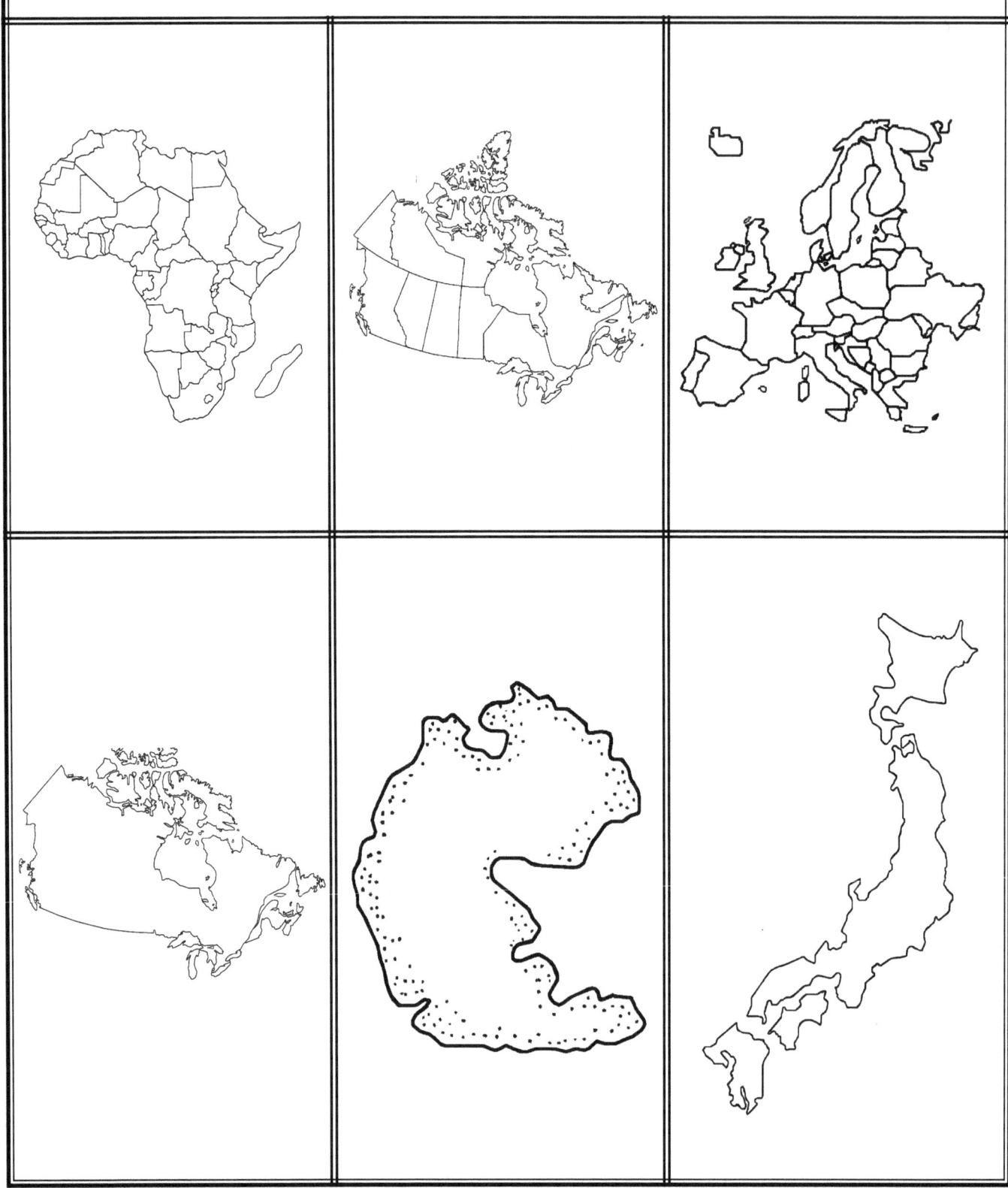

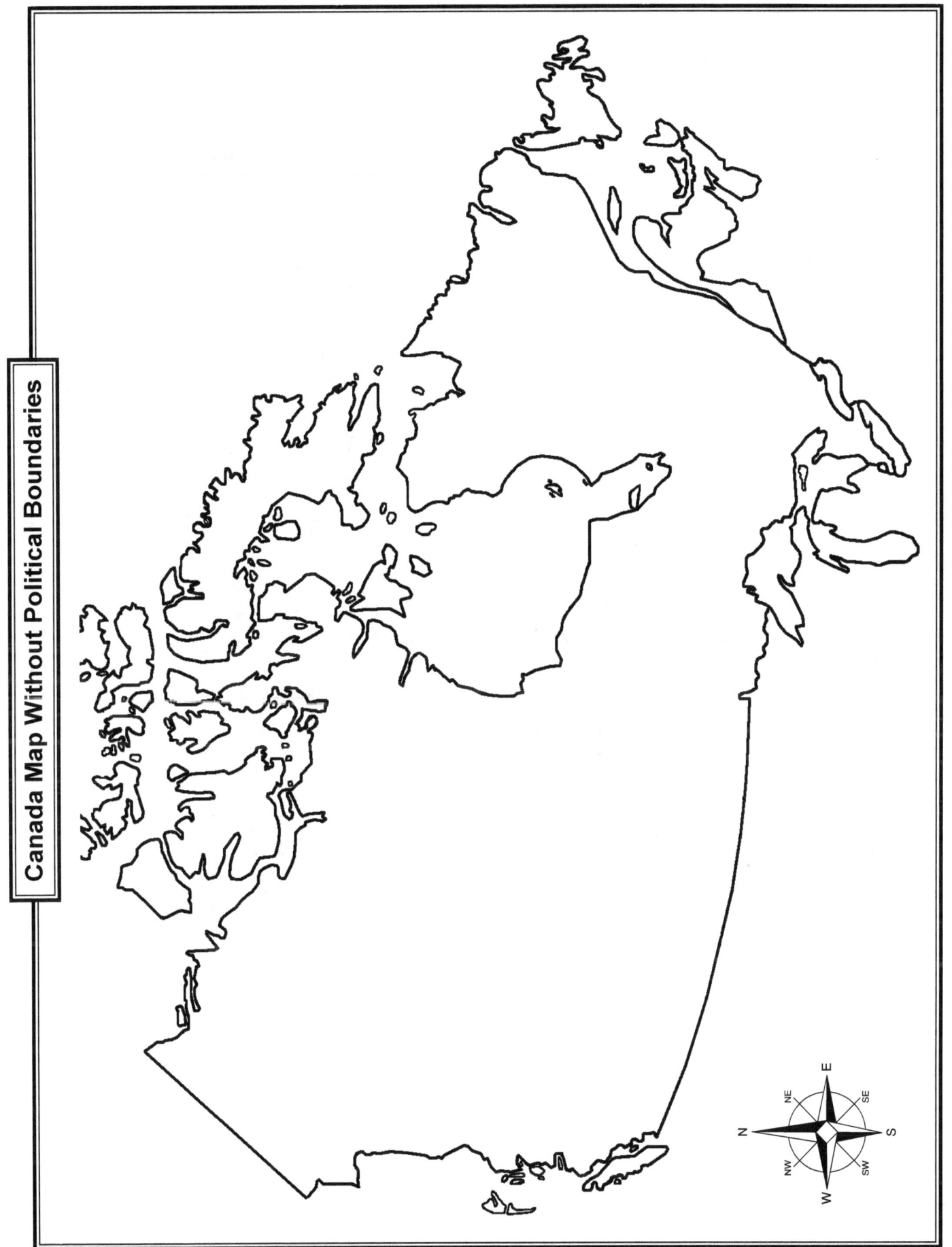

Canada on a Grid Map

Print the grid locations for the following:

1. Yellowknife _____
2. St. John's _____
3. Edmonton _____
4. Quebec City _____
5. Victoria _____
6. Iqaluit _____

Canada's Provinces and Territories

Legend
- ✶ capital city
- ✺ federal capital
- ○ city
- — province/territory

Provinces and Territories:
- Yukon — Whitehorse ✶
- Northwest Territories — Yellowknife ✶
- Nunavut — Iqaluit ✶
- British Columbia — Victoria ✶, Vancouver ○
- Alberta — Edmonton ✶, Calgary ○
- Saskatchewan — Regina ✶
- Manitoba — Winnipeg ✶, Churchill ○
- Ontario — Toronto ✶, Ottawa ✺
- Québec — Québec City ✶, Montreal ○
- Newfoundland & Labrador — St. John's ✶
- Prince Edward Island — Charlottetown ✶
- Nova Scotia — Halifax ✶
- New Brunswick — Fredericton ✶

Compass rose: N, NE, E, SE, S, SW, W, NW

SSJ1-79 ISBN: 9781554951031   15 © S&S Learning Materials

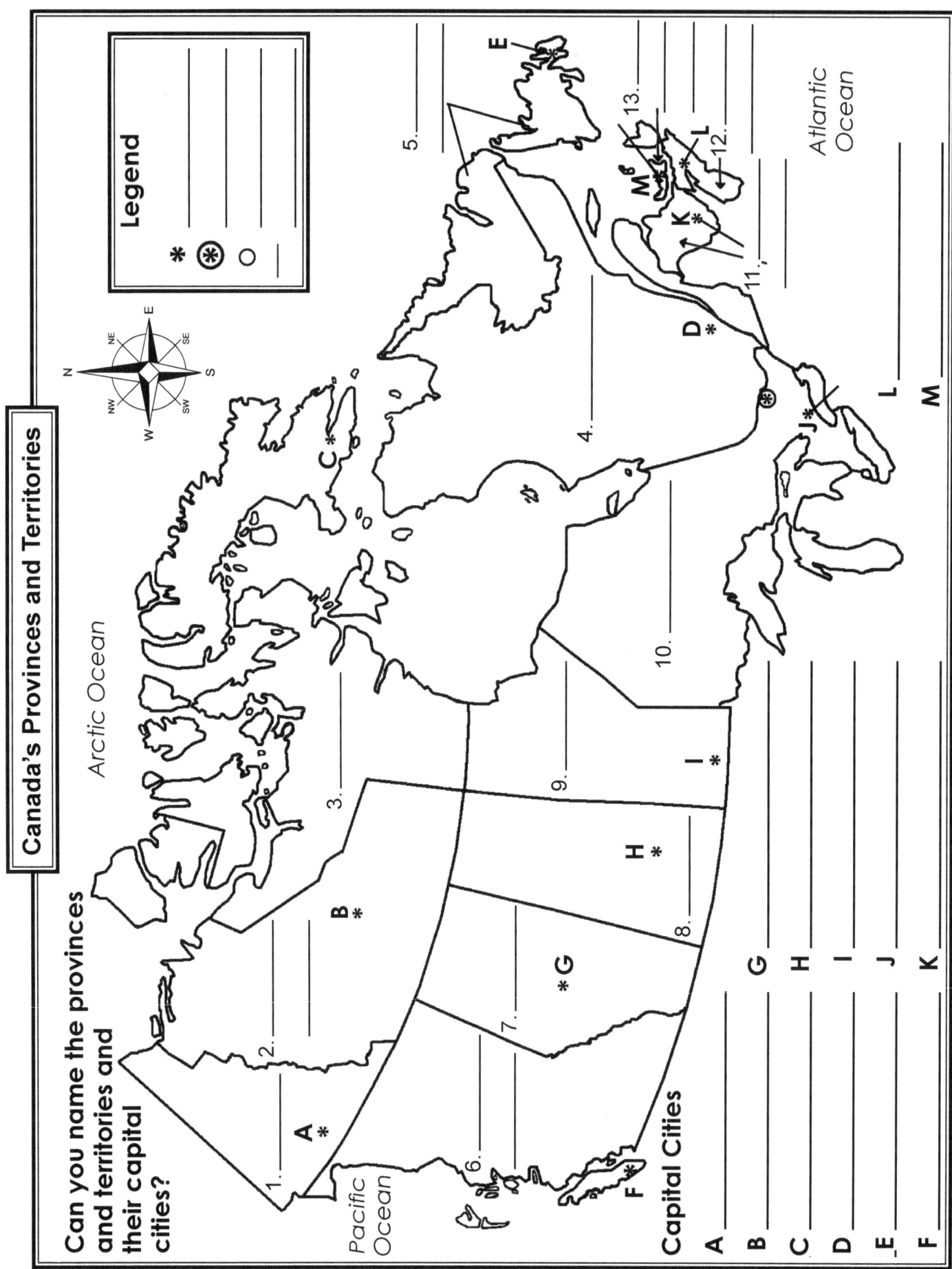

Colours on a Map

Colours on a map help us to see and find the places very well.

Colour the most westerly province green.

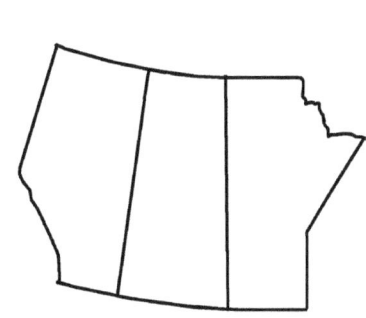
Colour the prairie provinces (plains) yellow.

Colour the most westerly territory red

Colour the most easterly province grey.

Colour Canada's largest territory blue.

Colour the Maritime provinces pink.

Colour the province with the Great Lakes purple

Colour the largest province orange

Colour the territory north of Alberta brown.

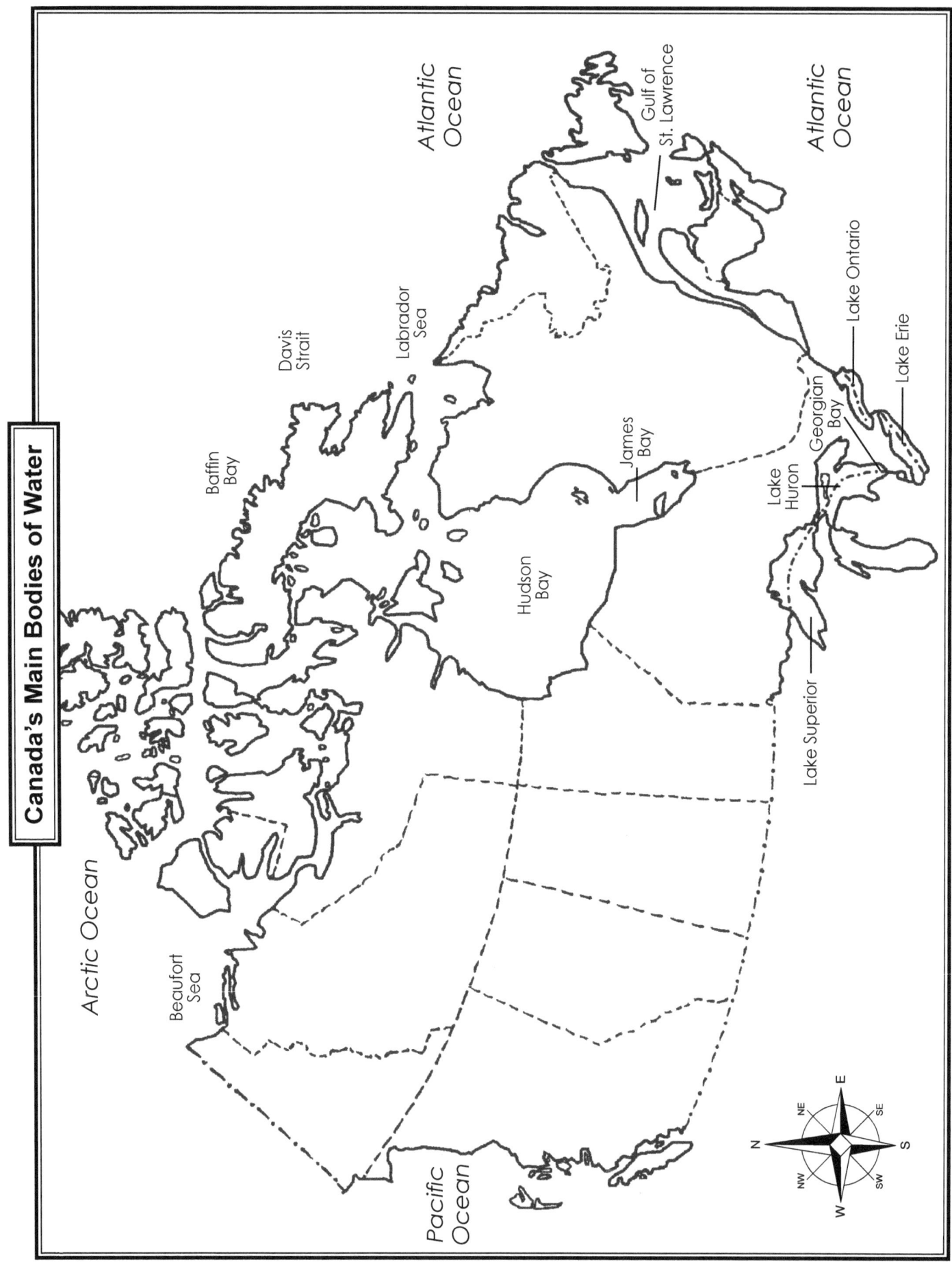

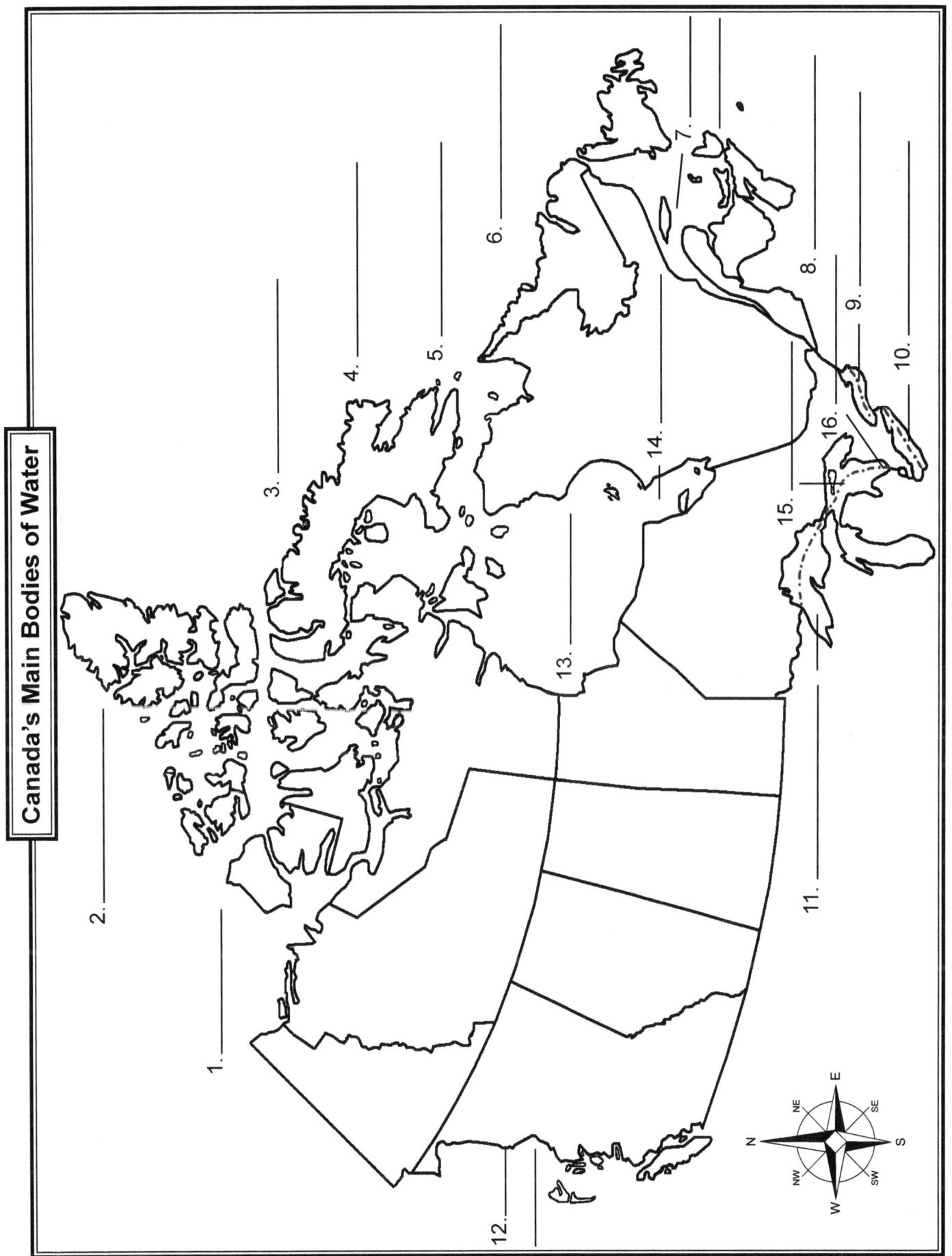

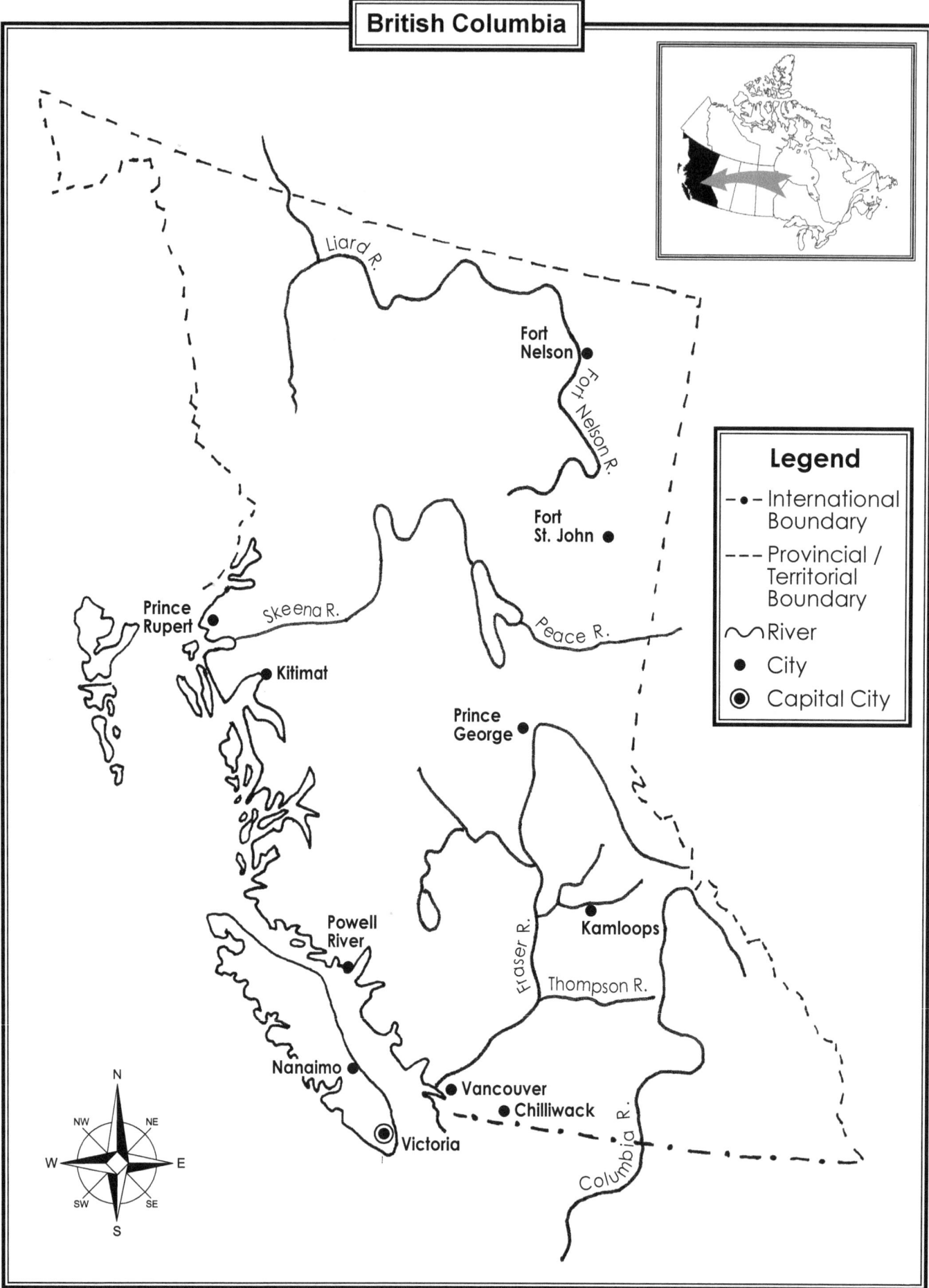

British Columbia

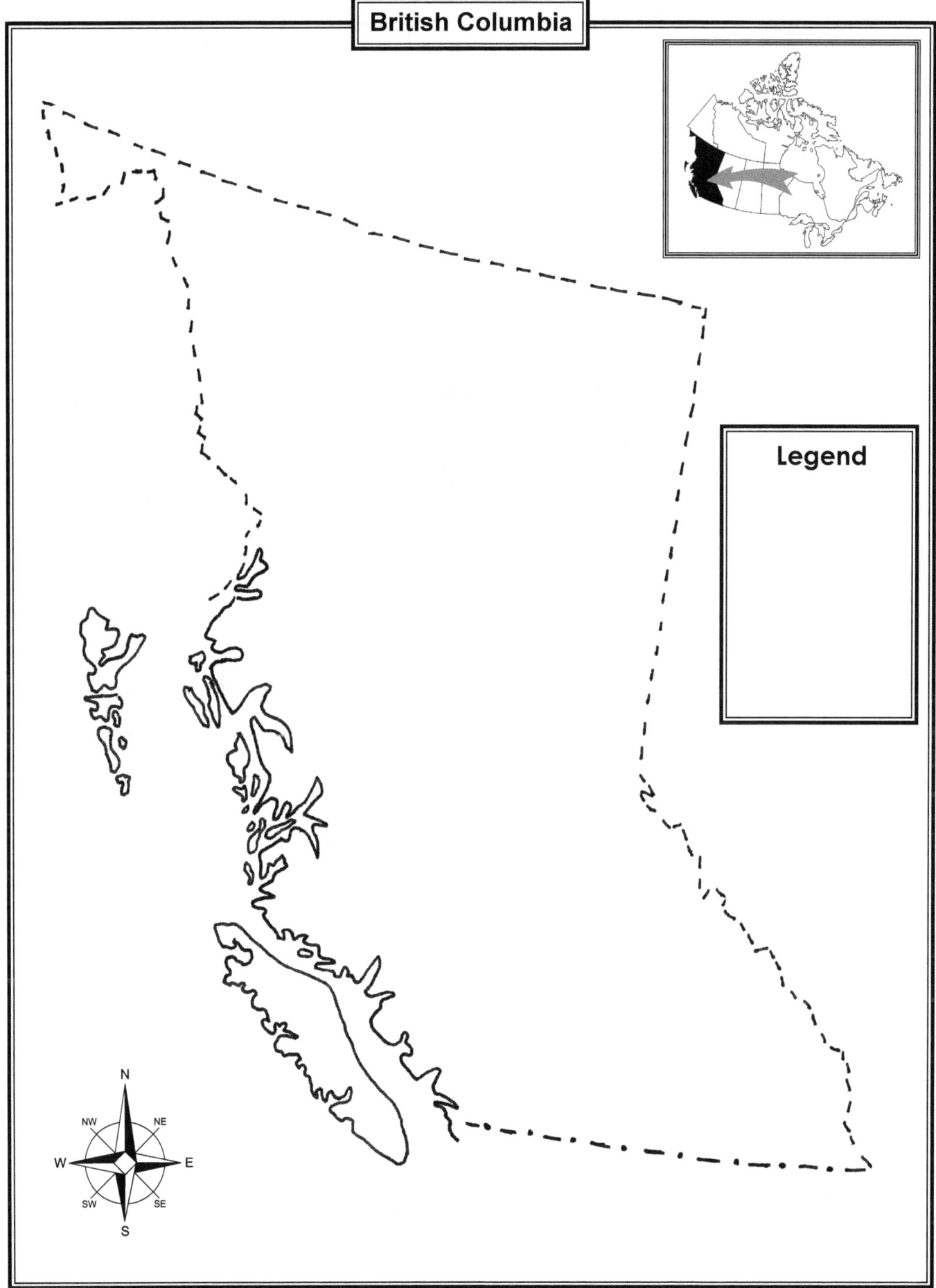

Alberta

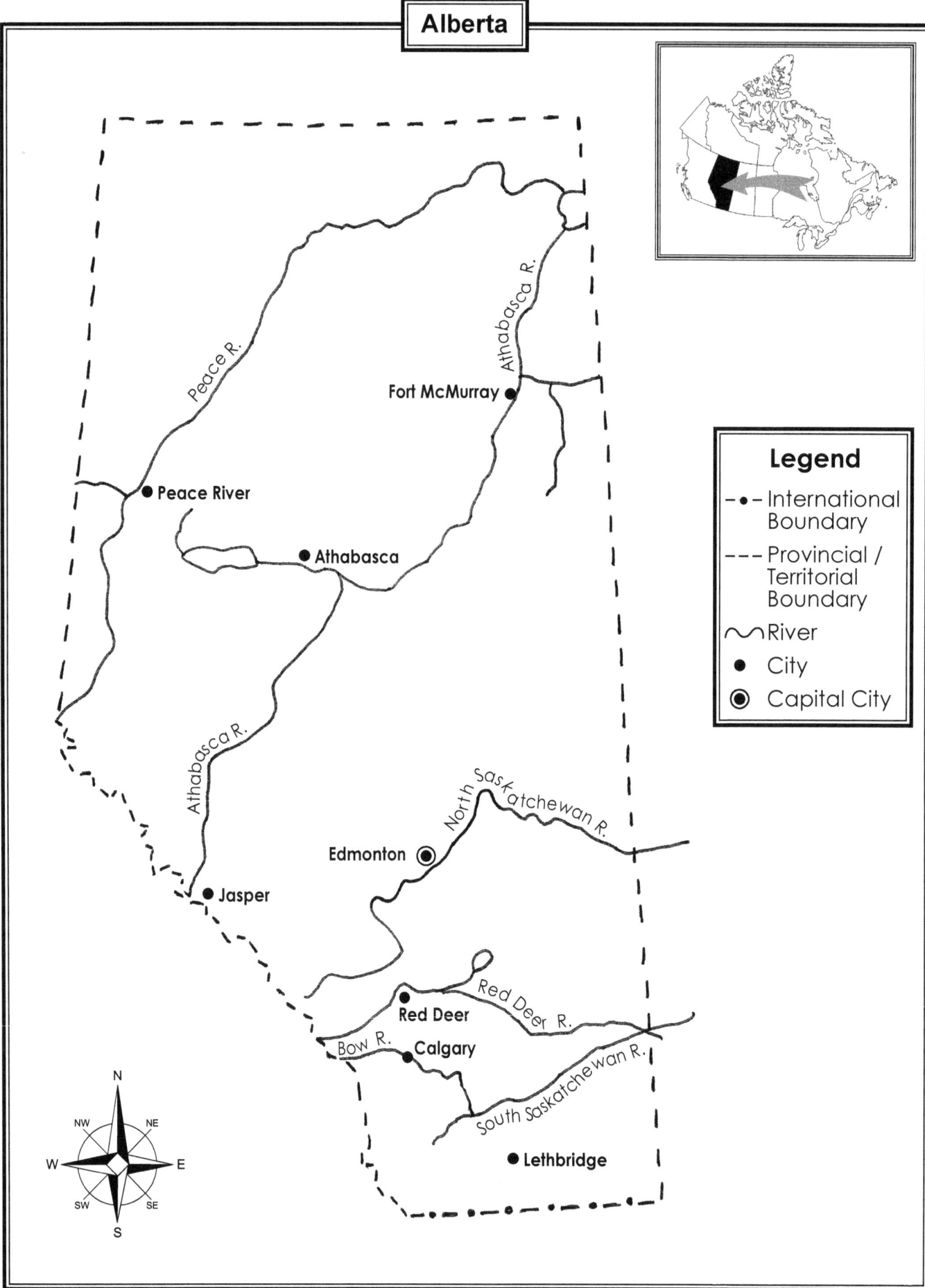

Alberta

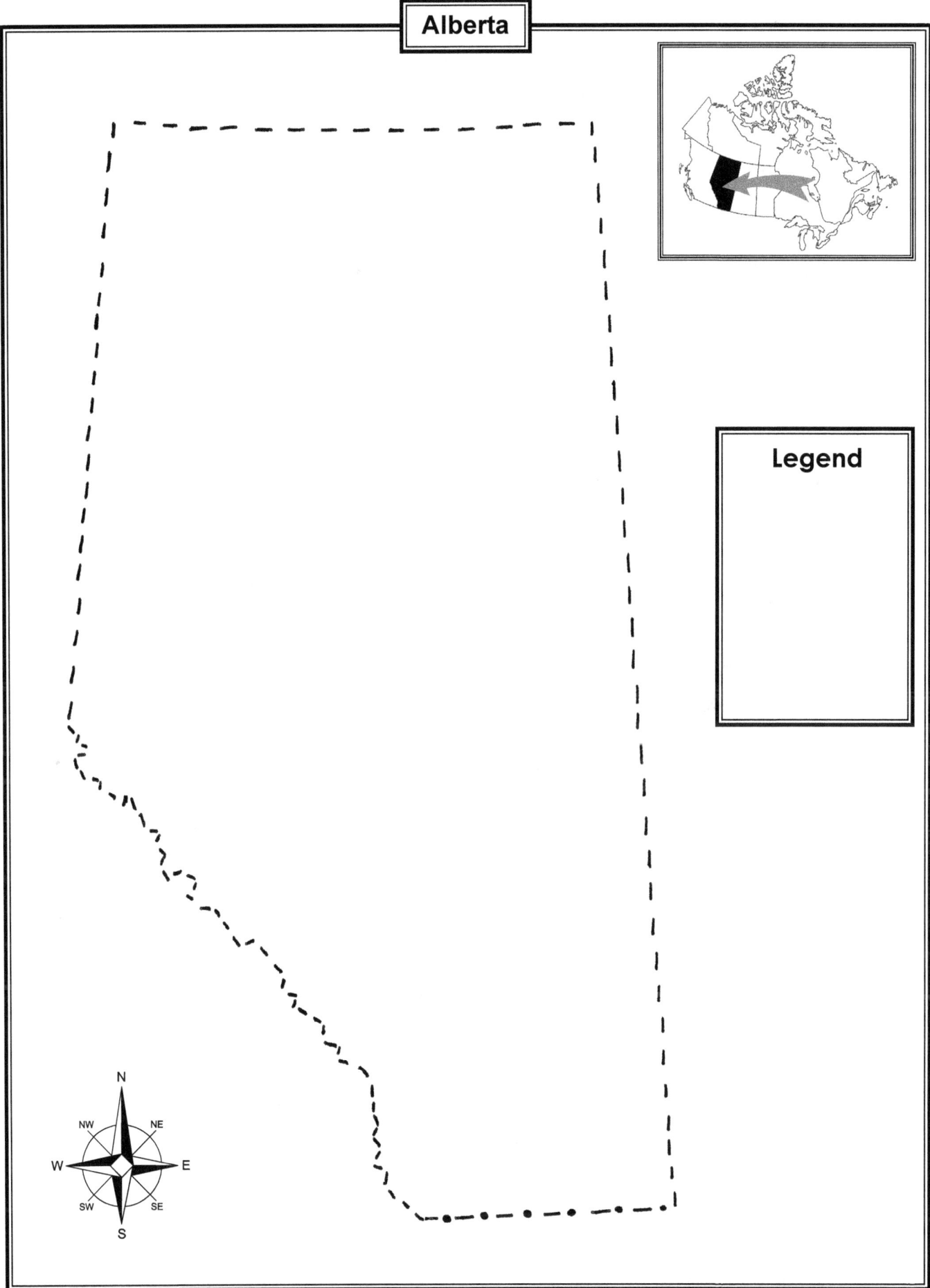

Legend

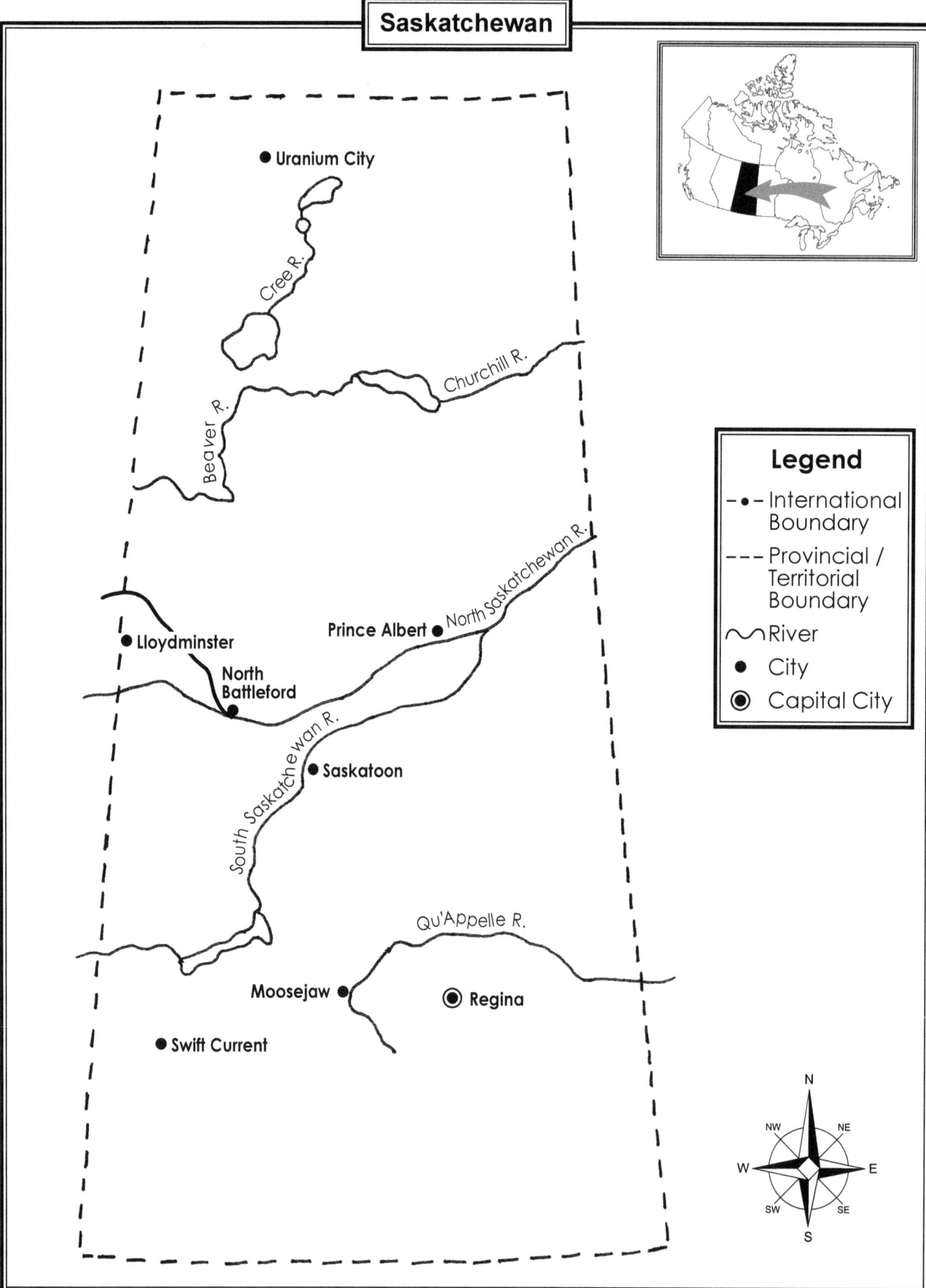

Saskatchewan

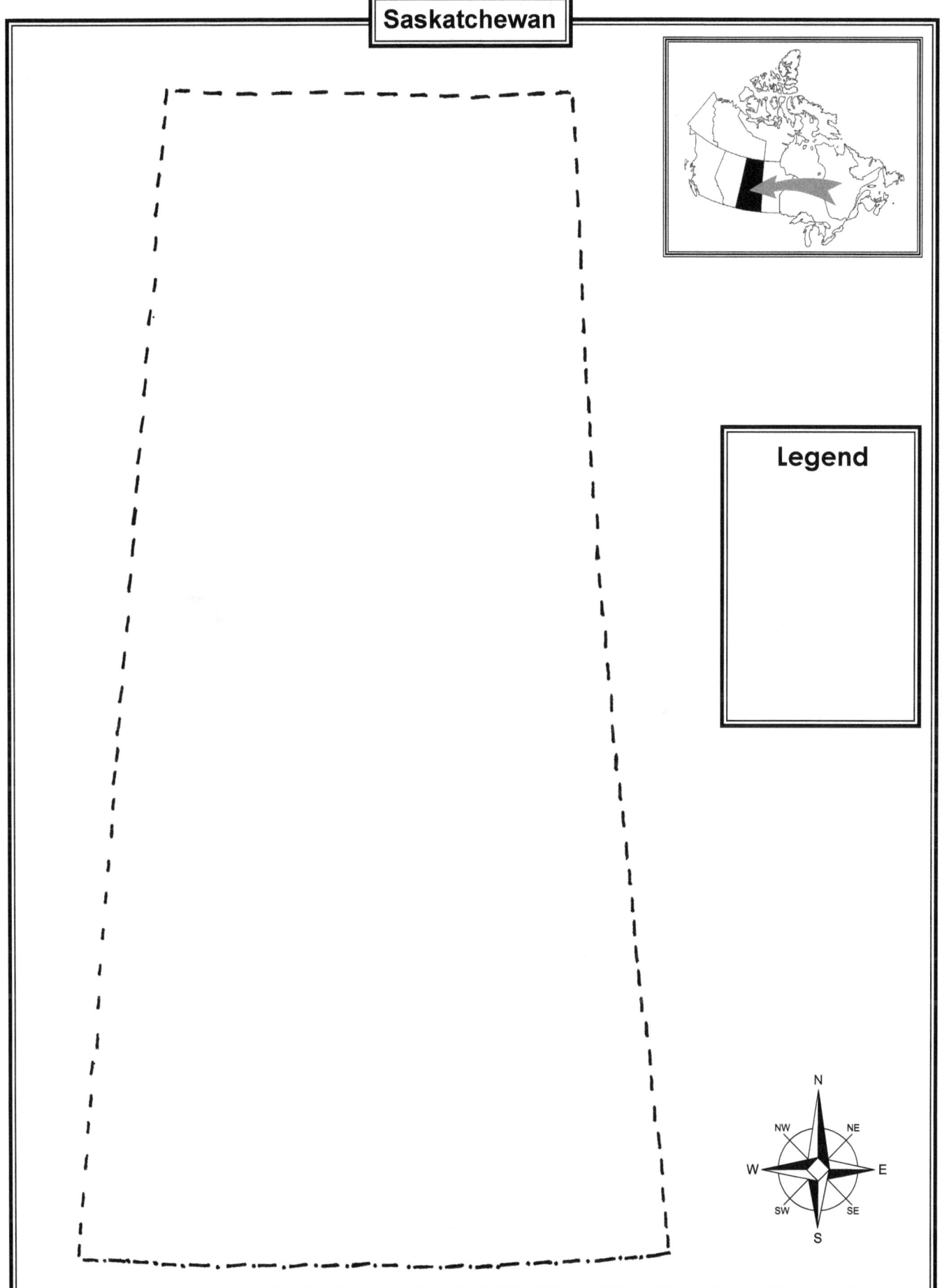

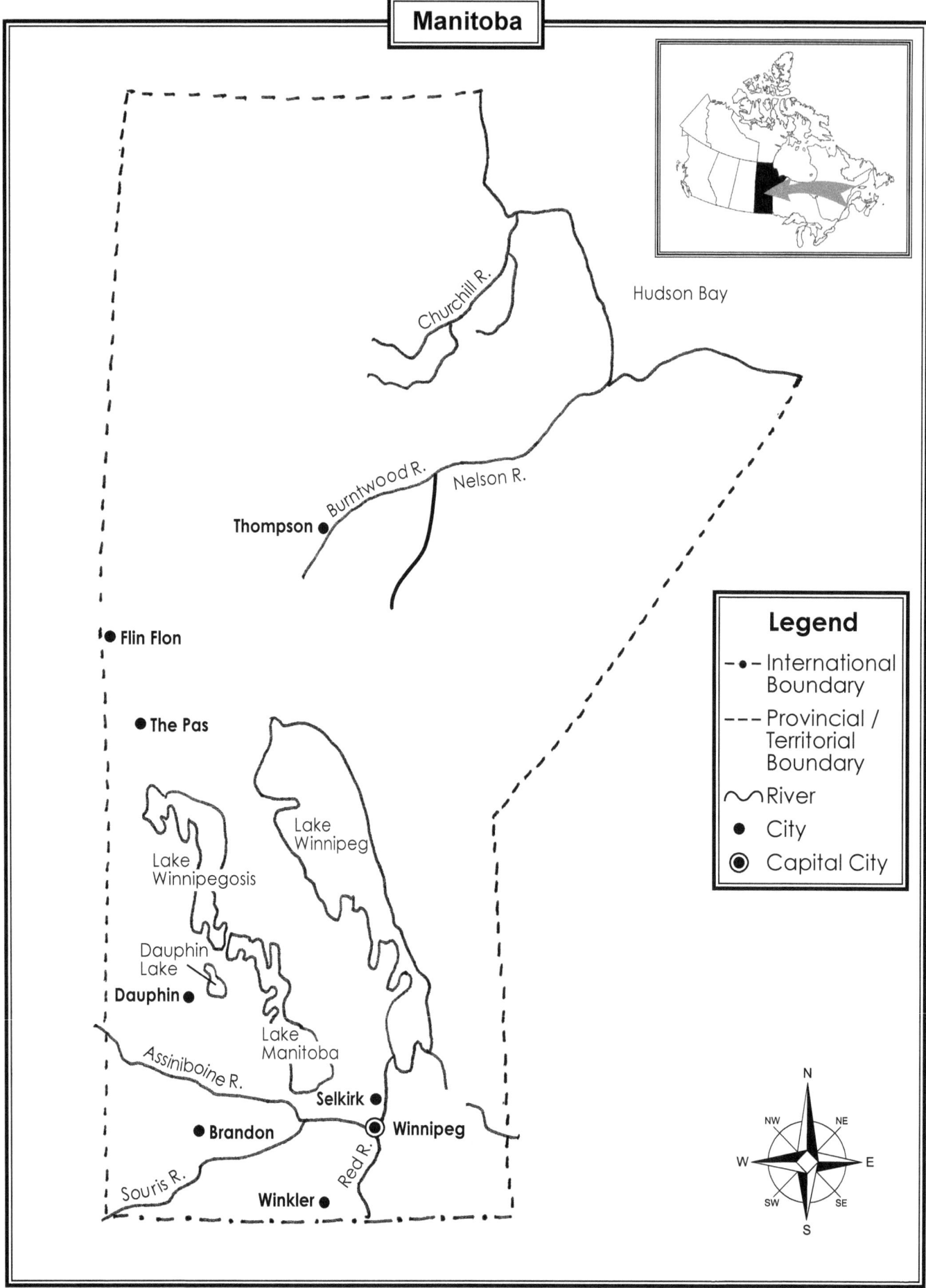

Manitoba

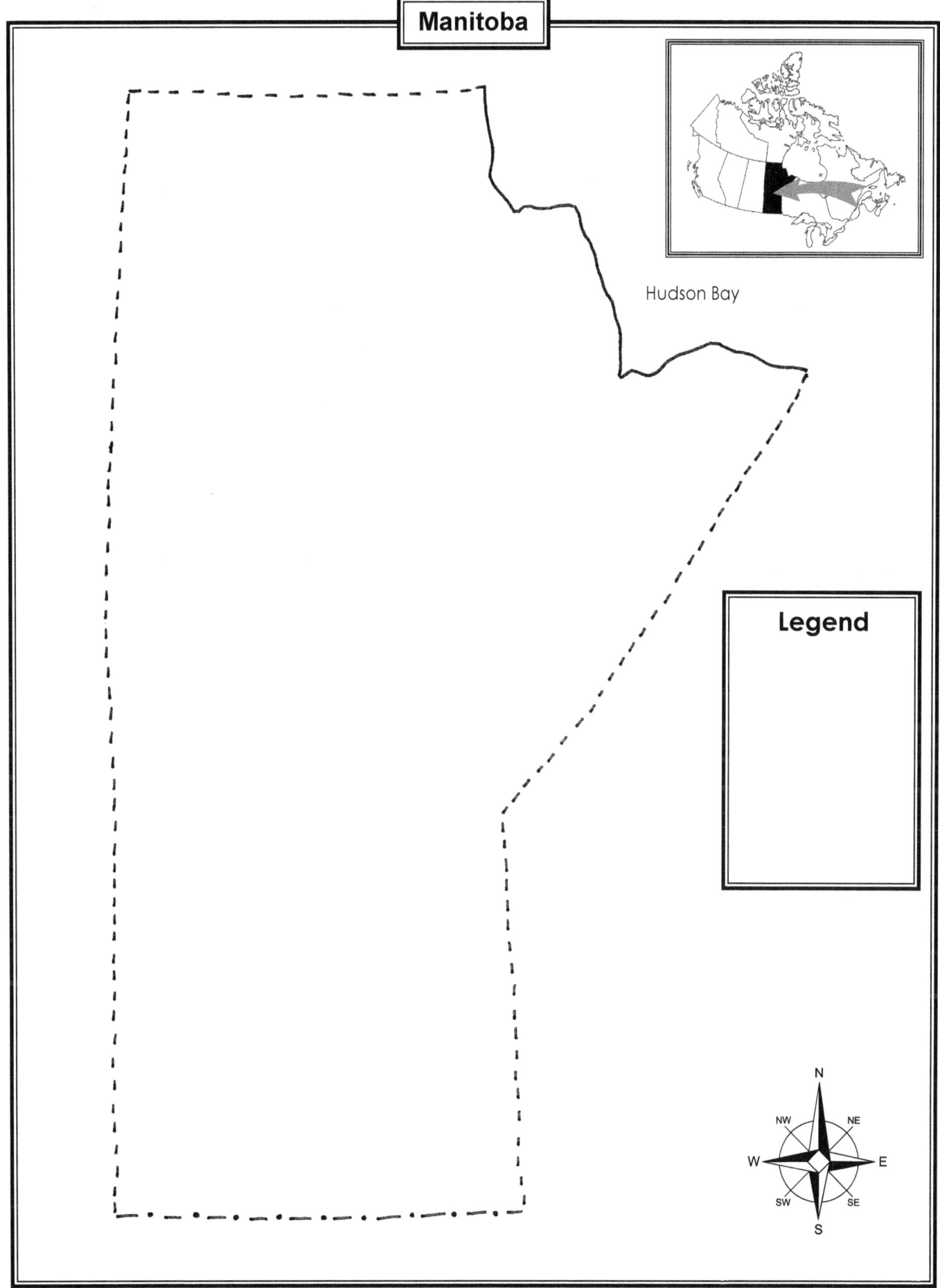

Hudson Bay

Legend

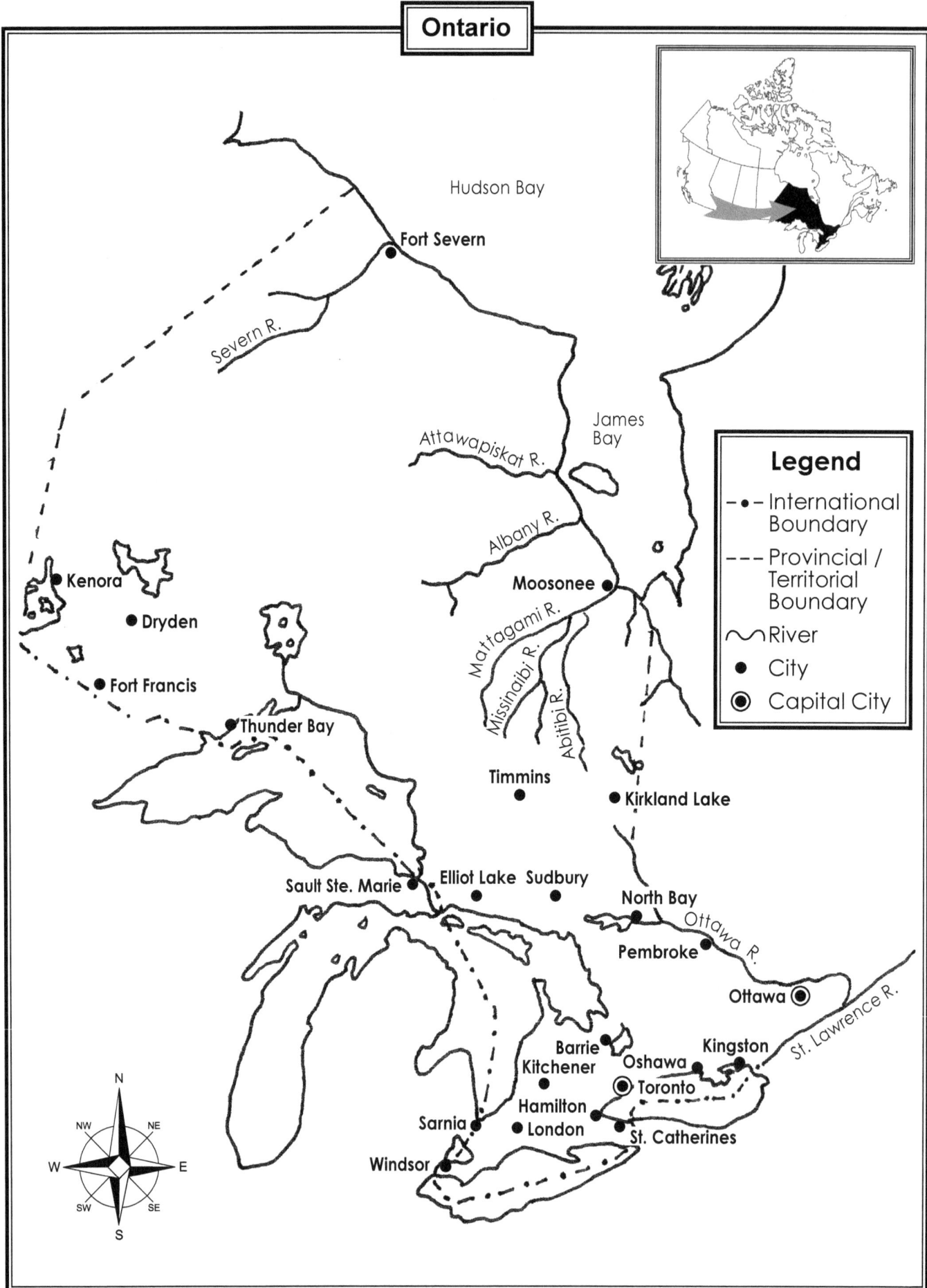

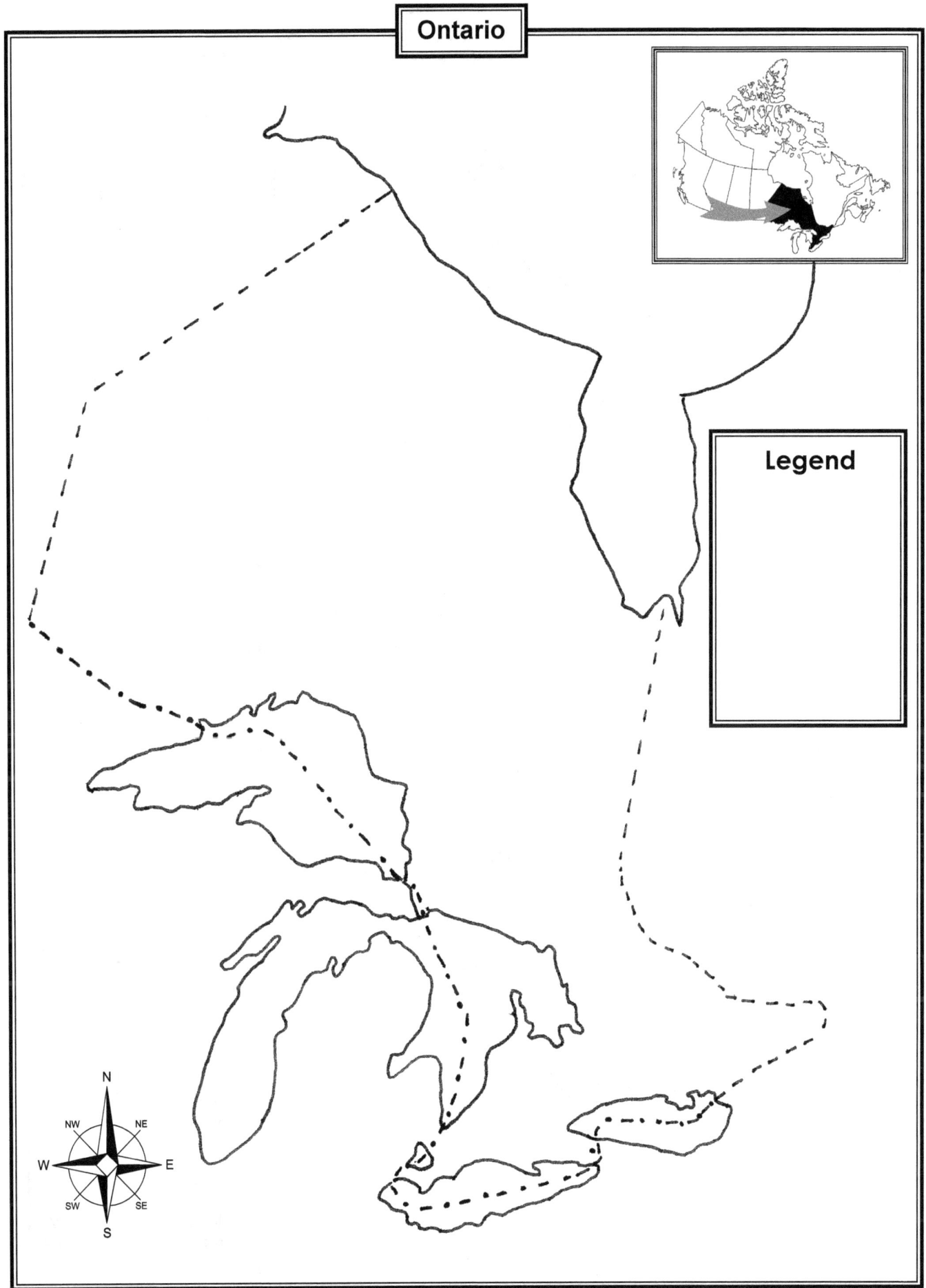

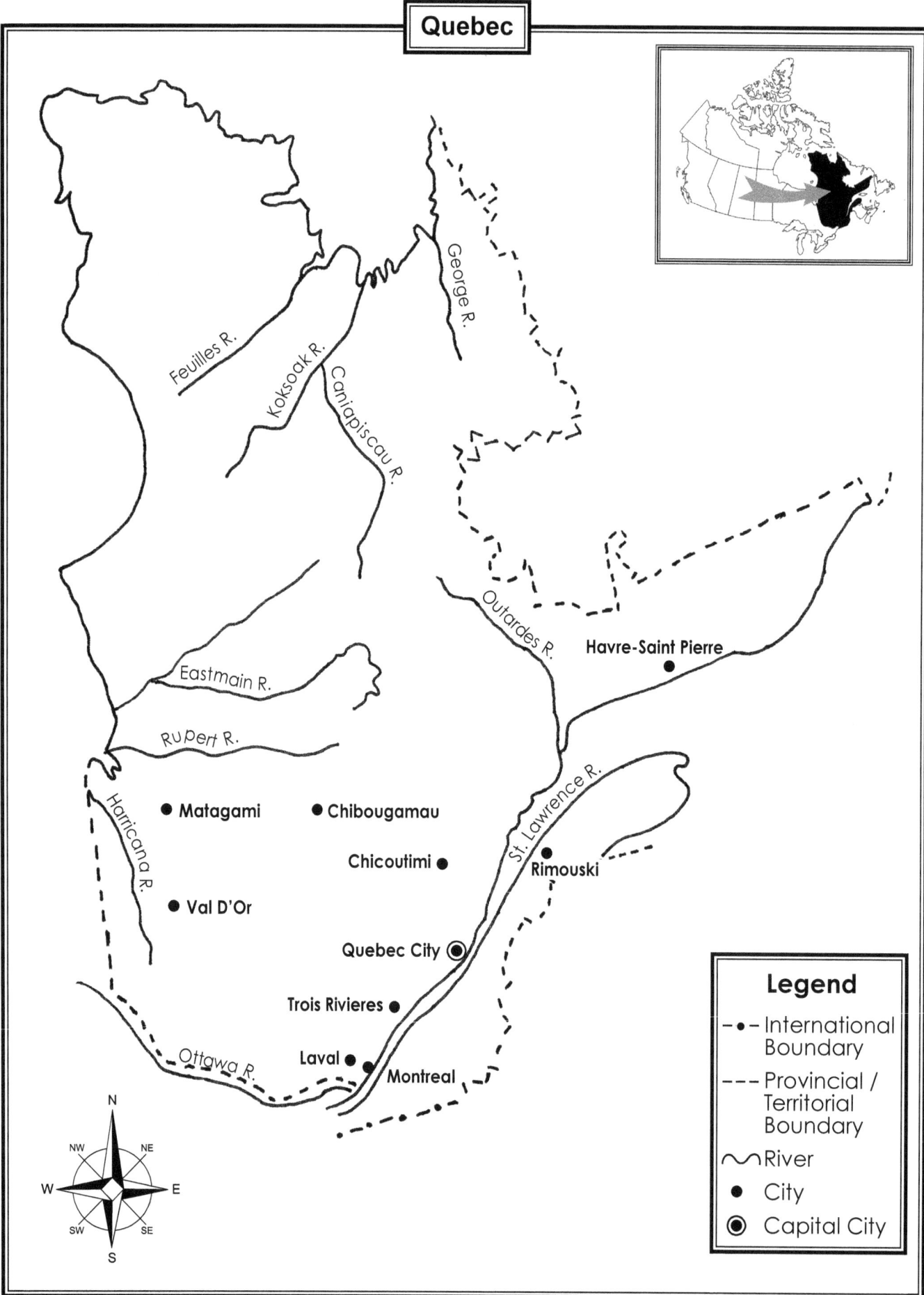

Quebec

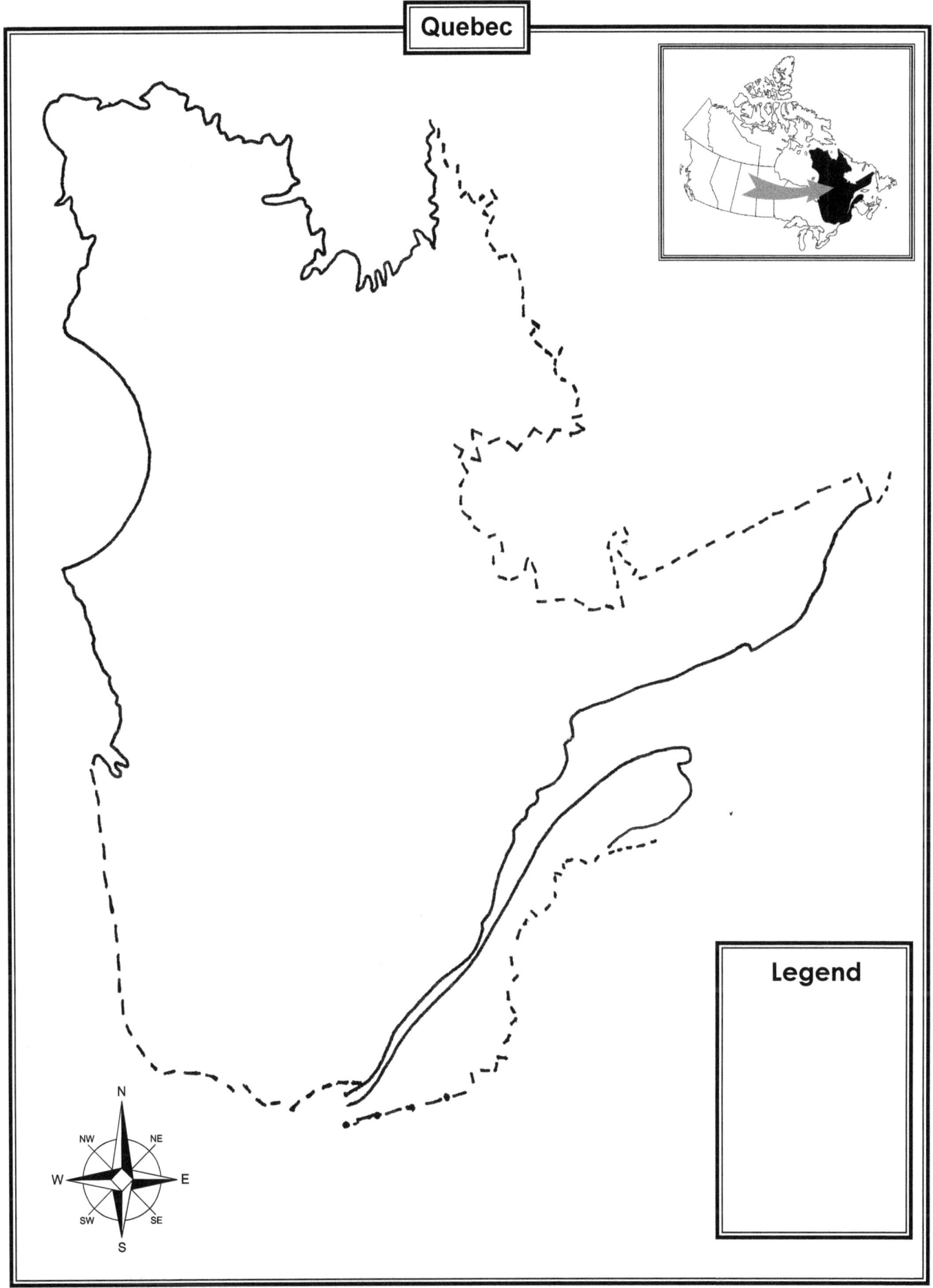

Legend

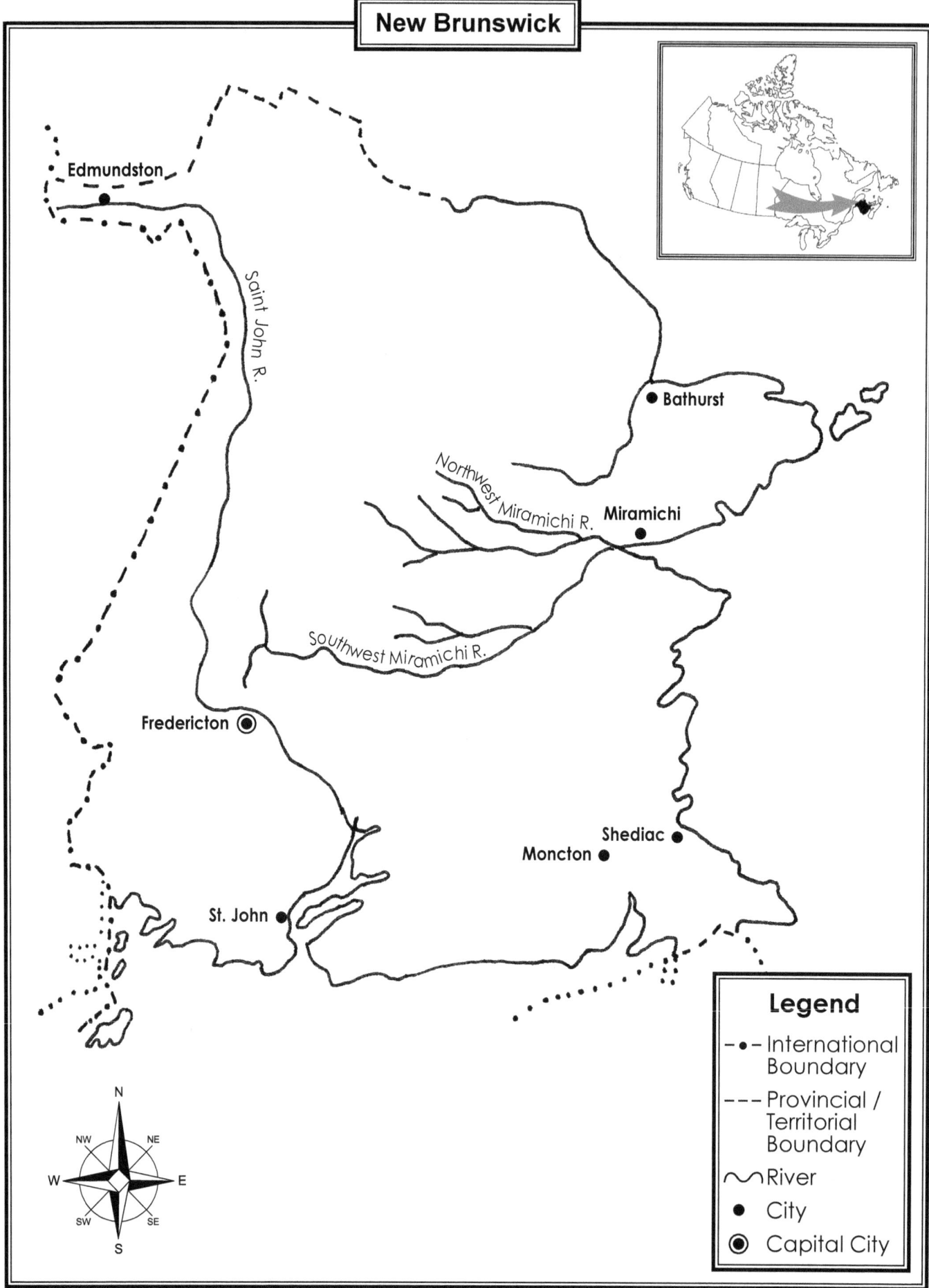

New Brunswick

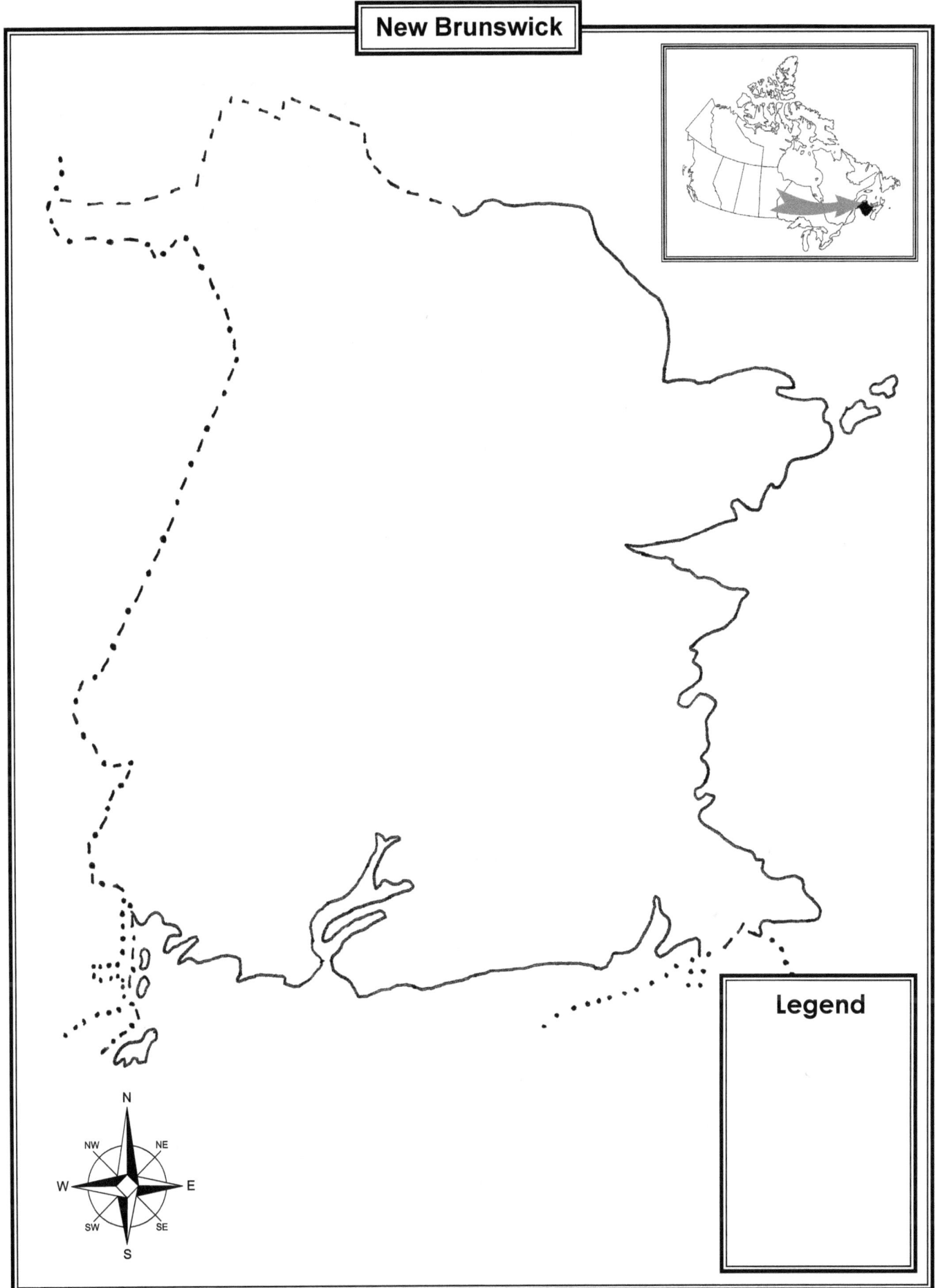

Legend

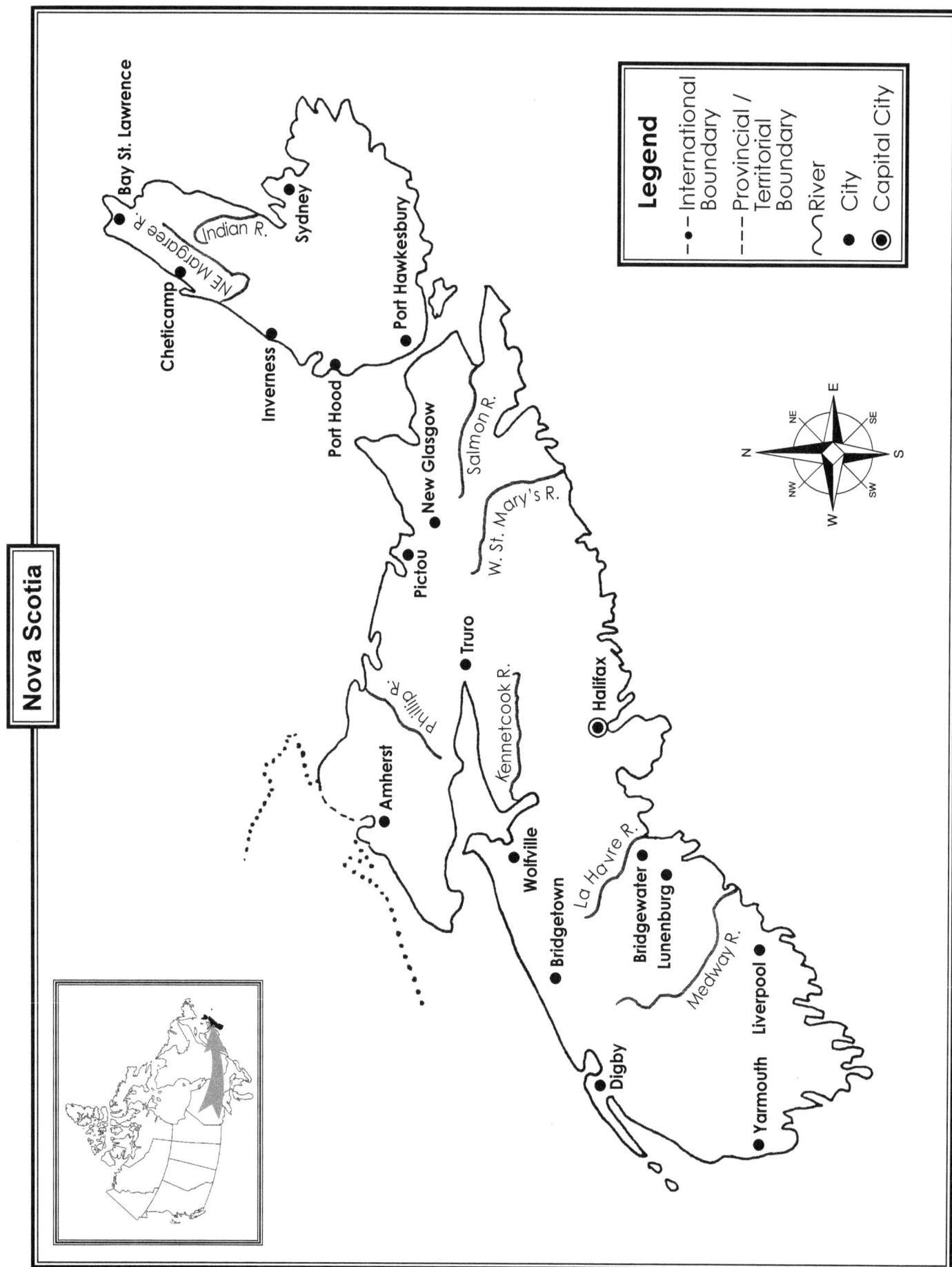

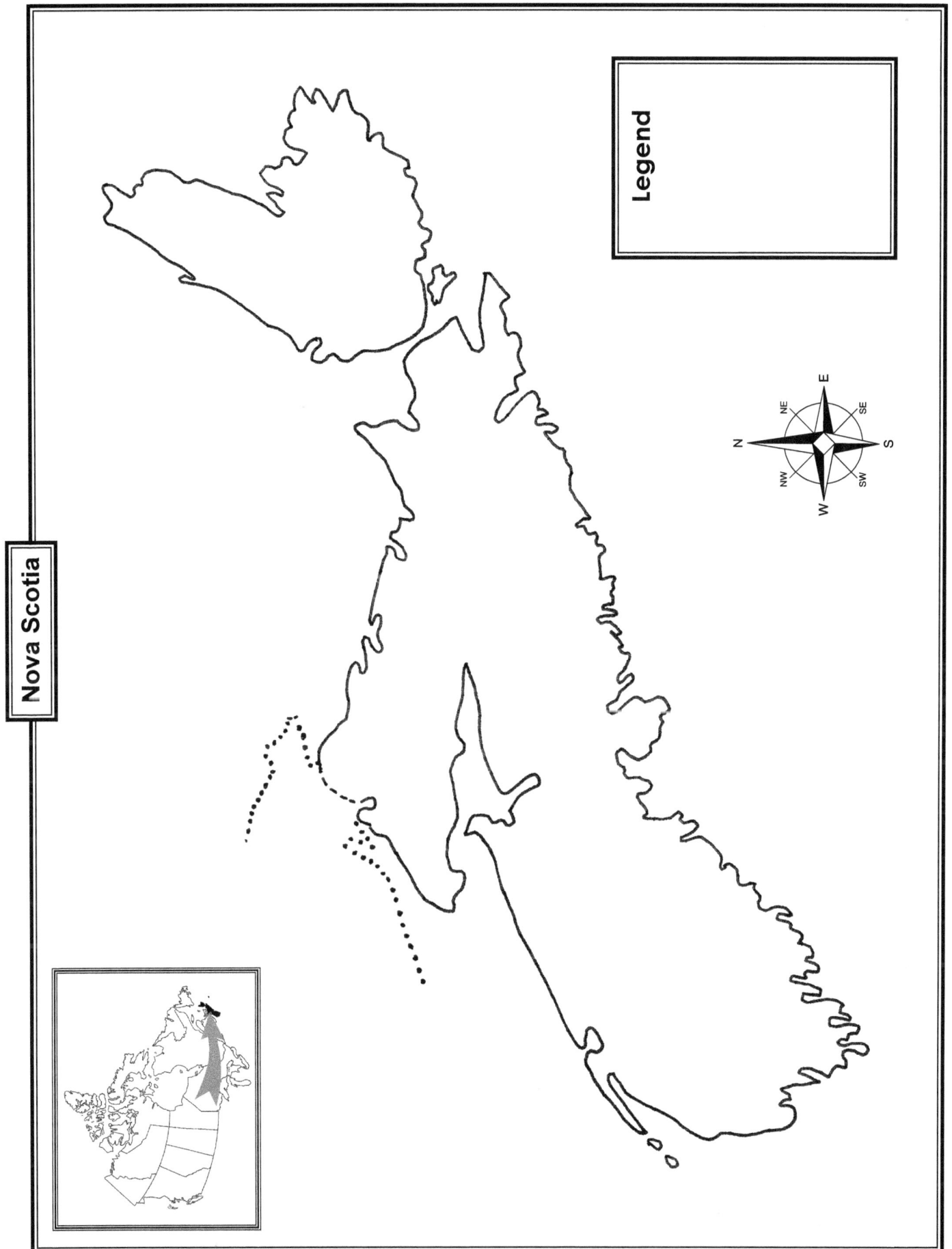

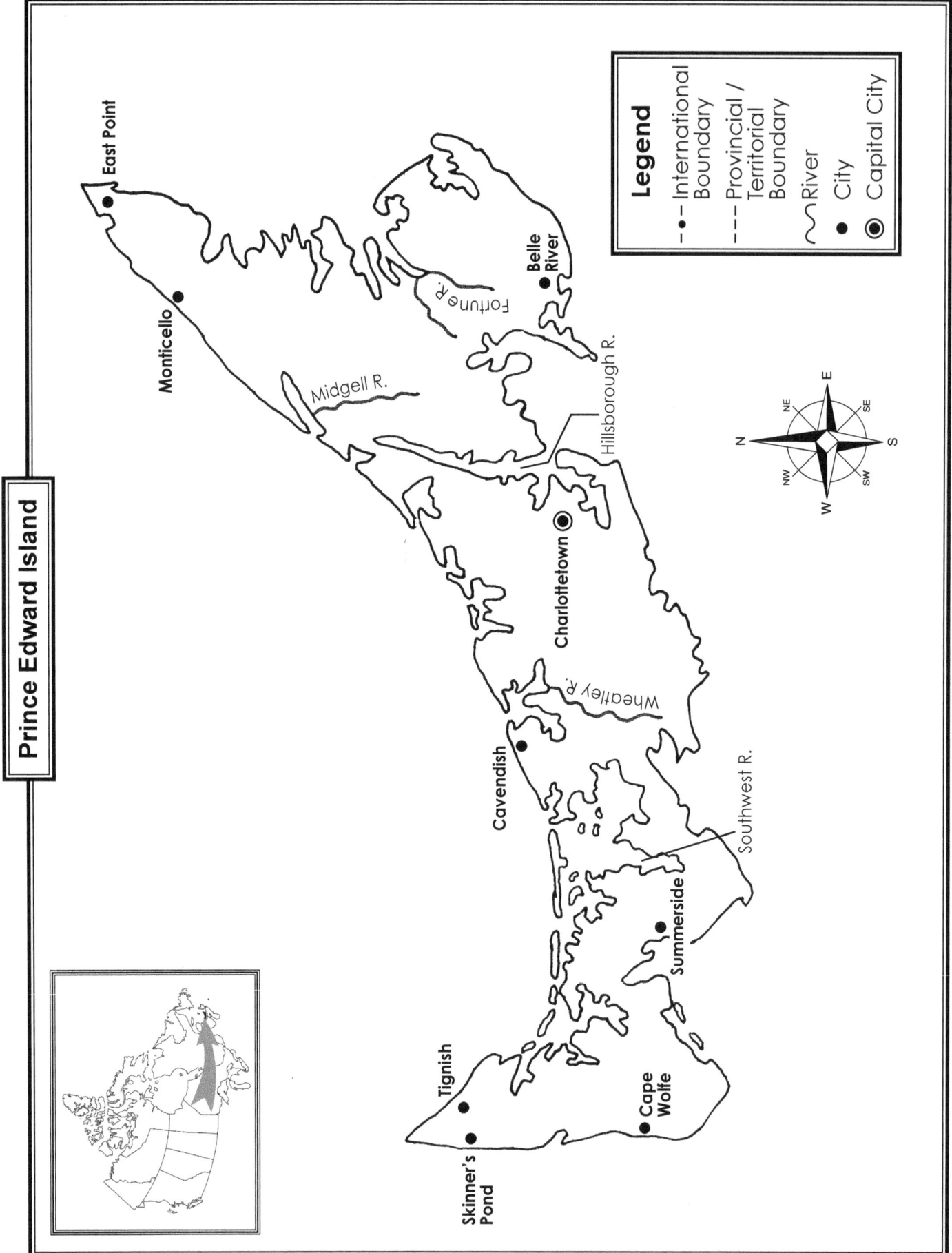

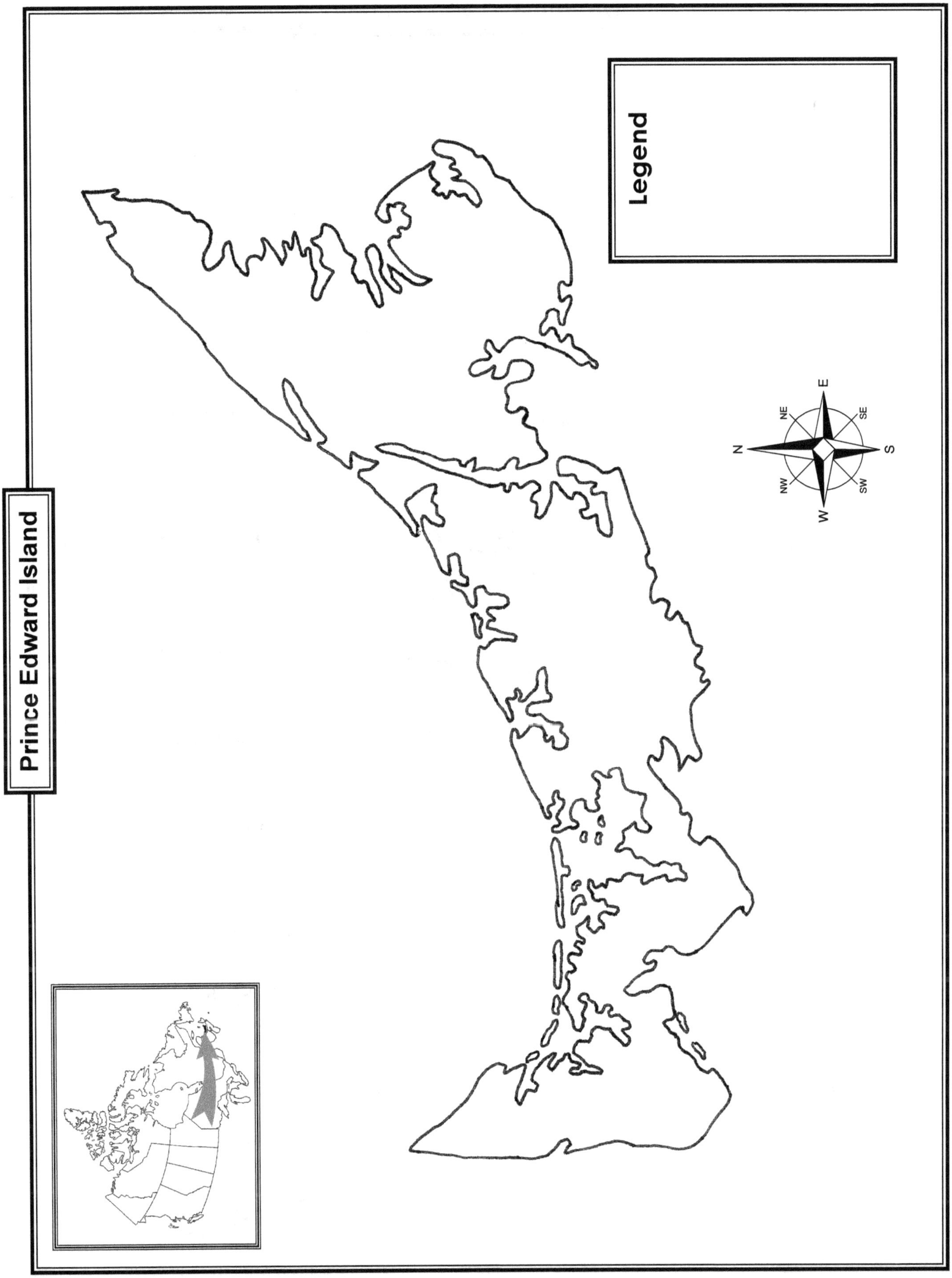

Prince Edward Island

Legend

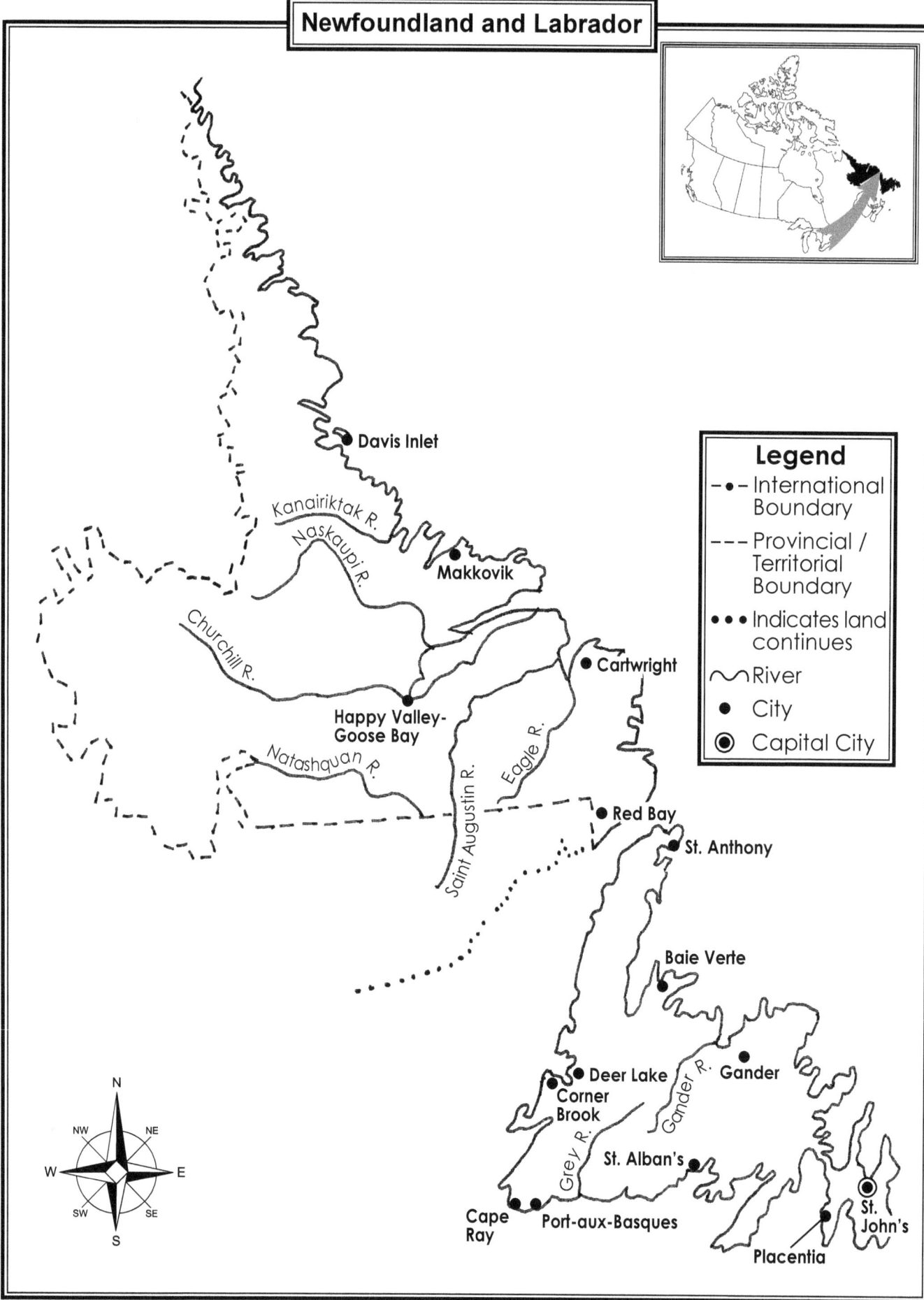

Newfoundland and Labrador

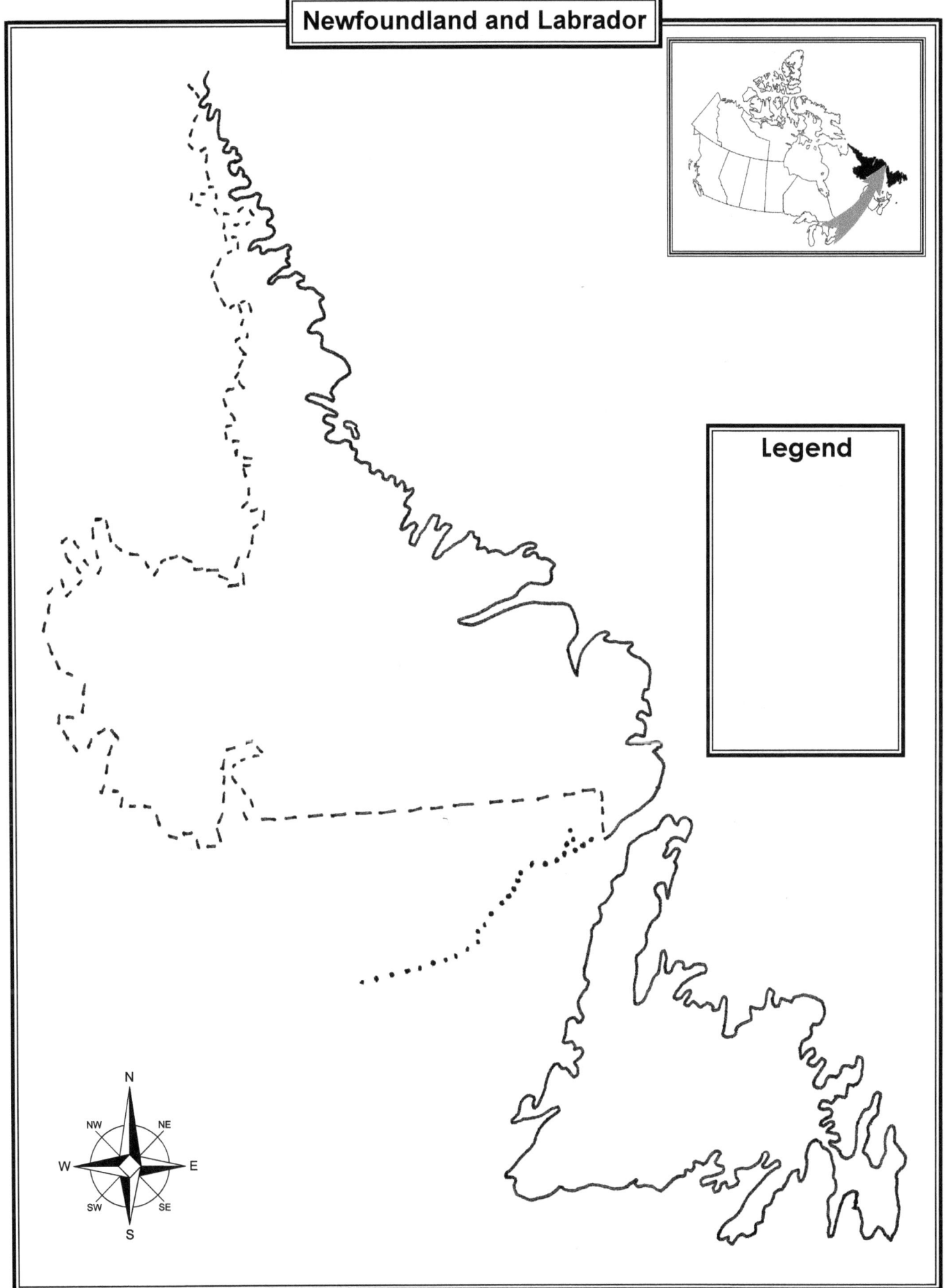

Legend

Nunavut

Nunavut

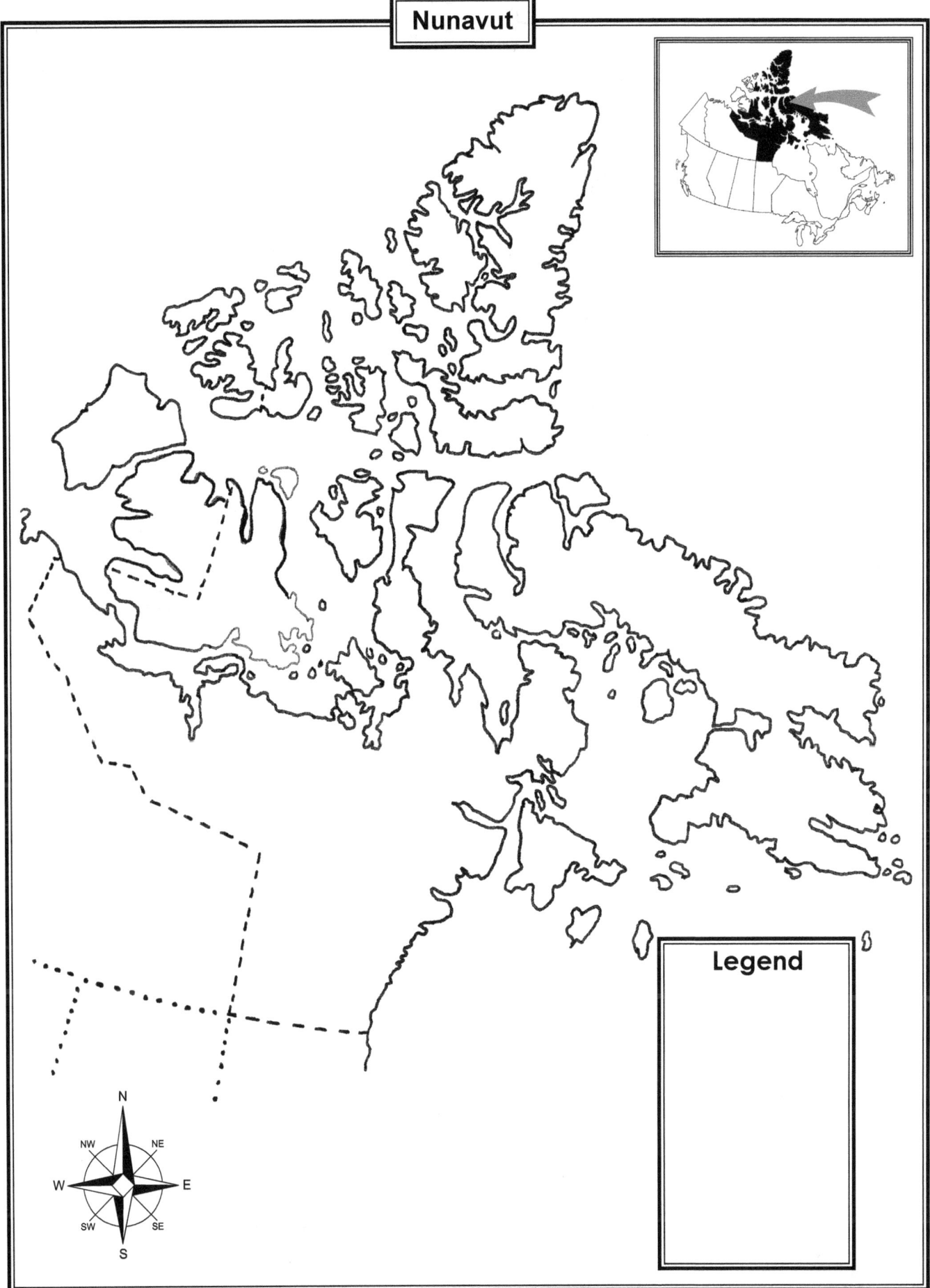

Legend

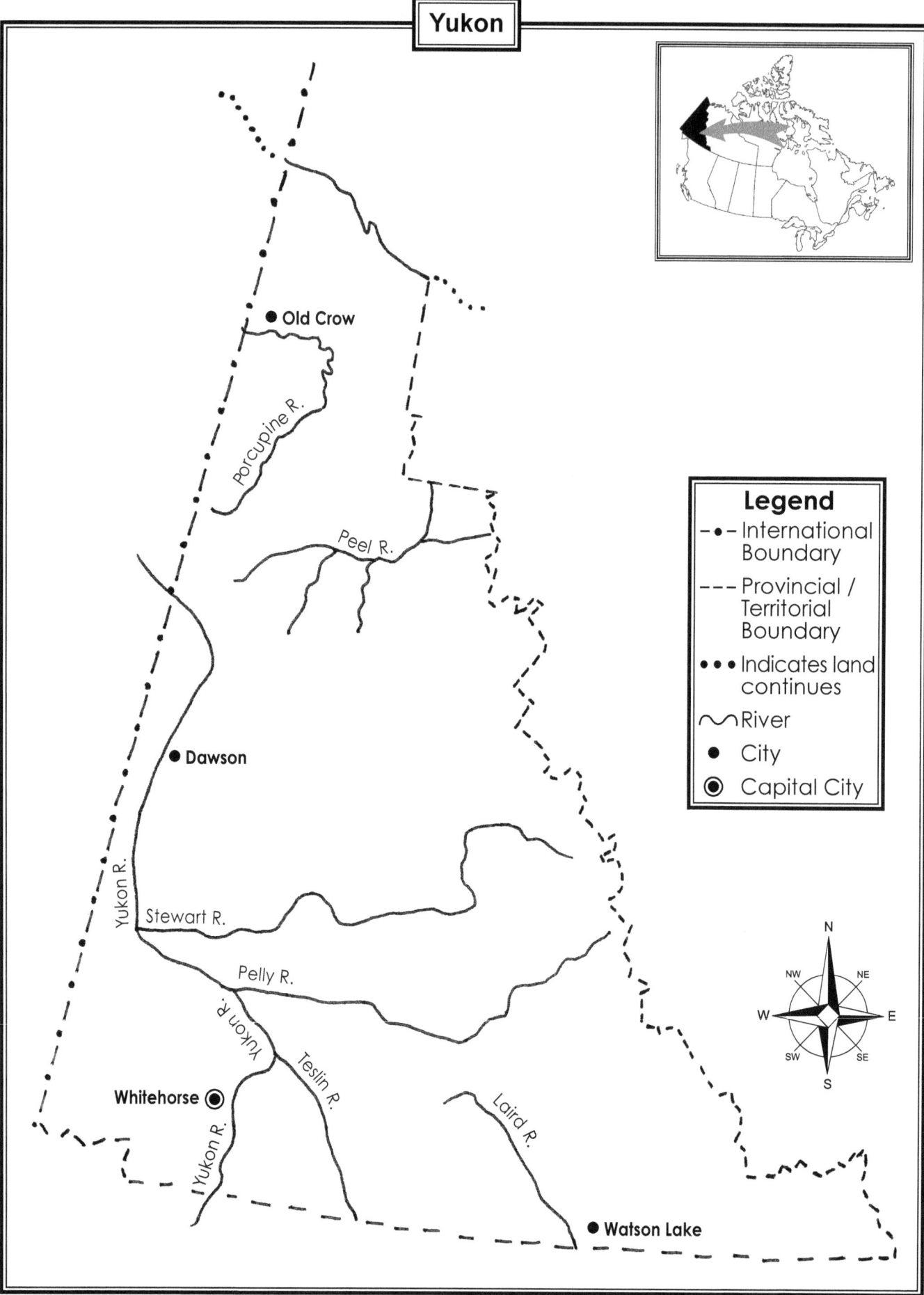

Yukon

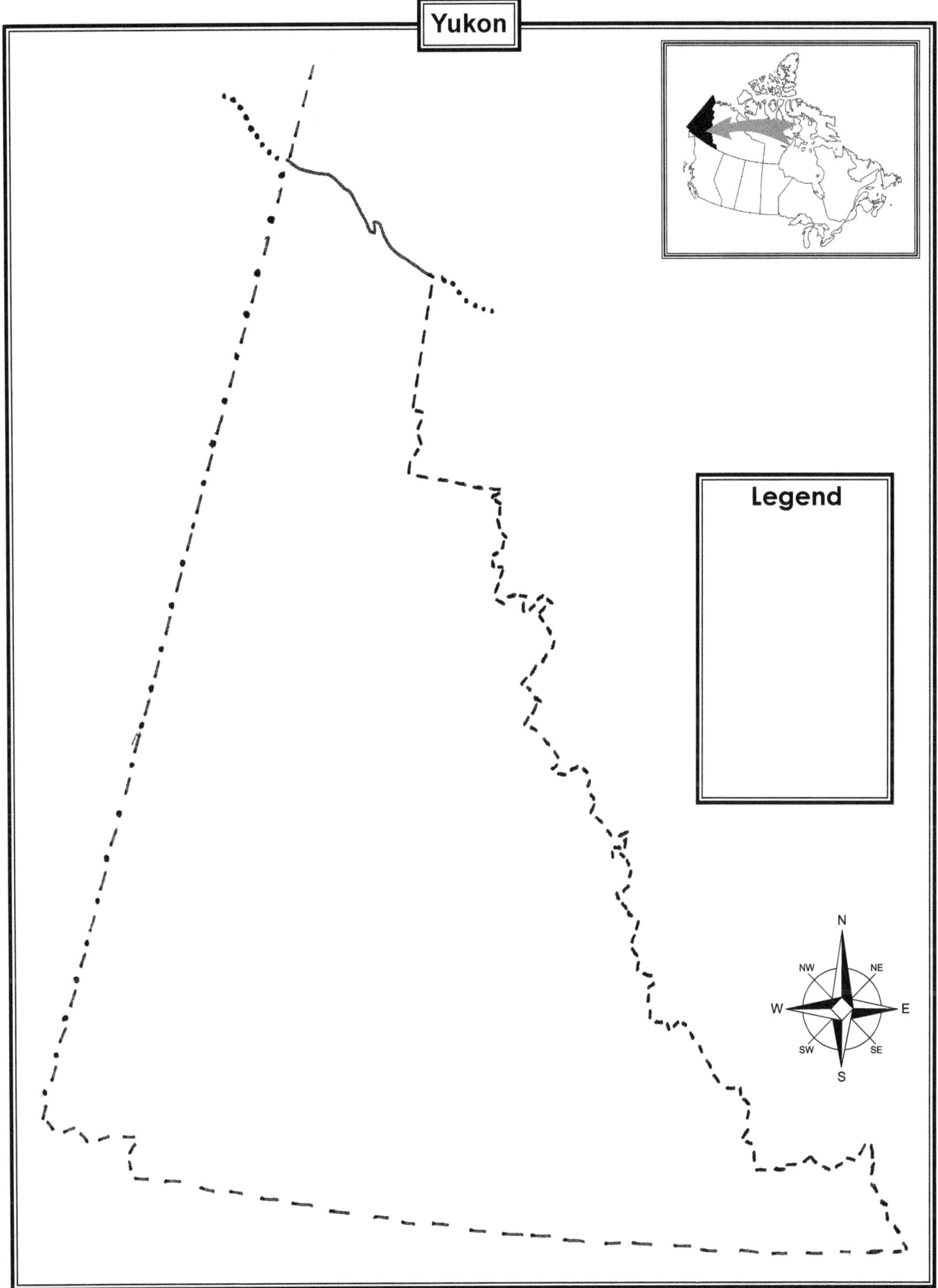

Northwest Territories

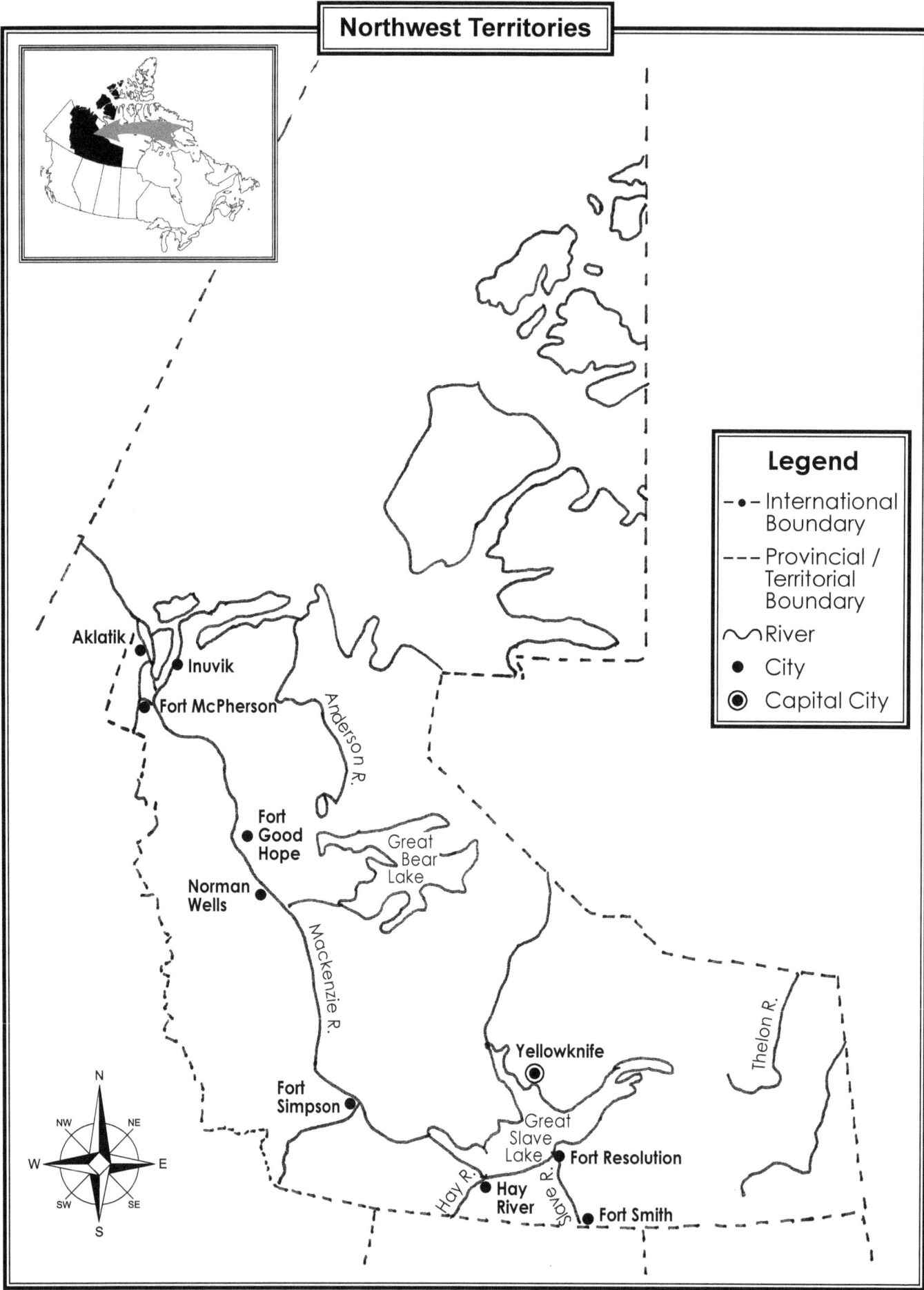

Northwest Territories

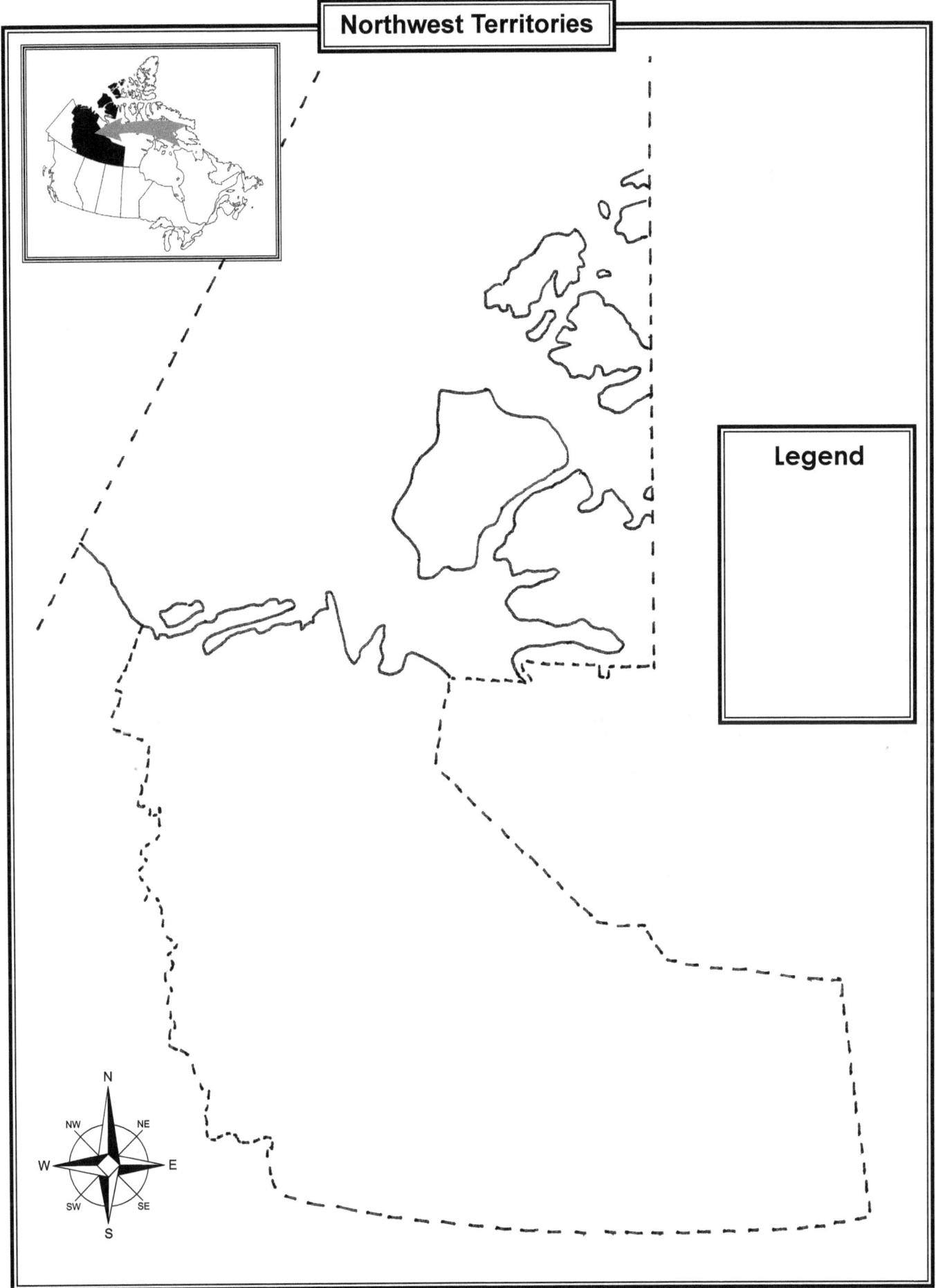

Legend

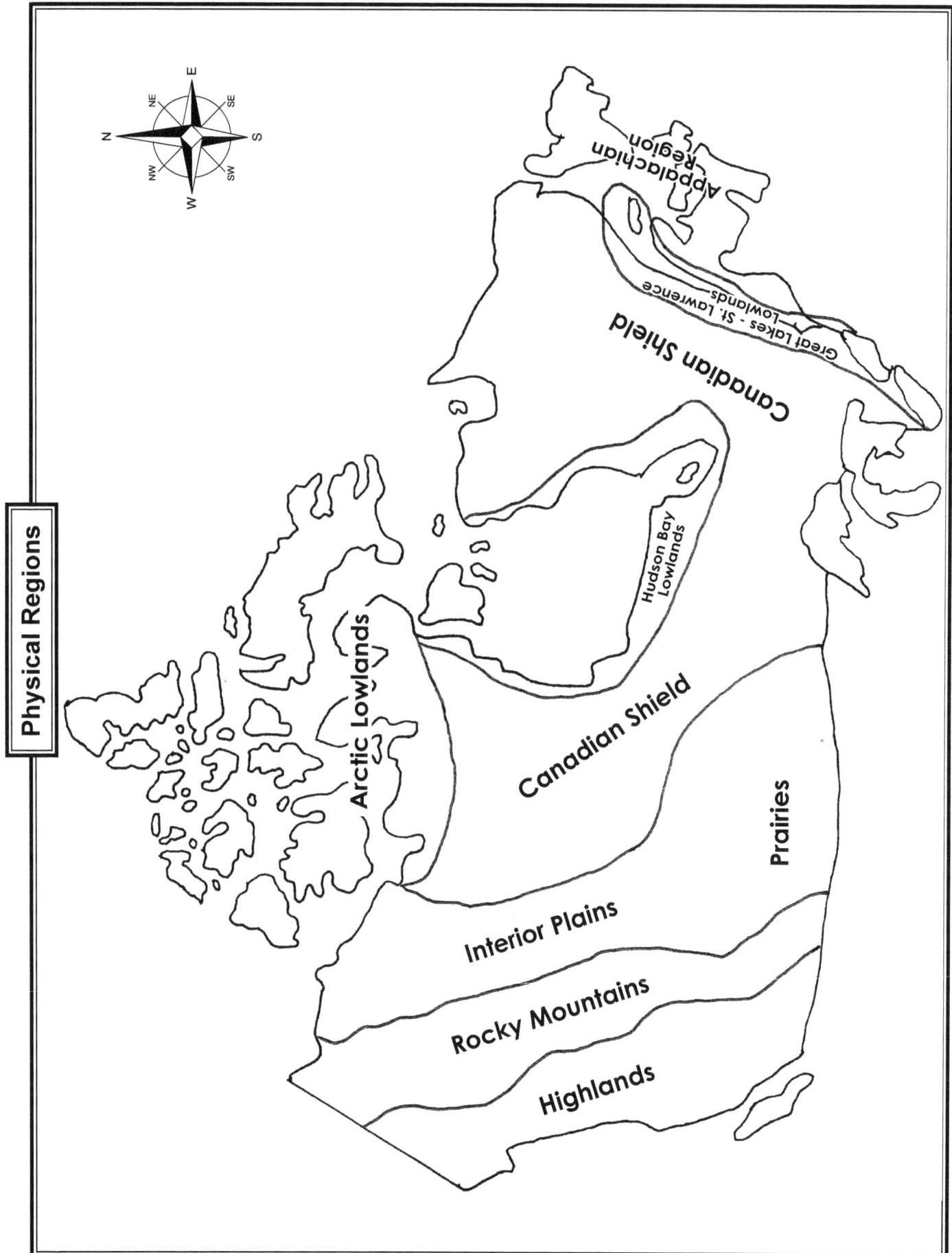

Northwest Territories

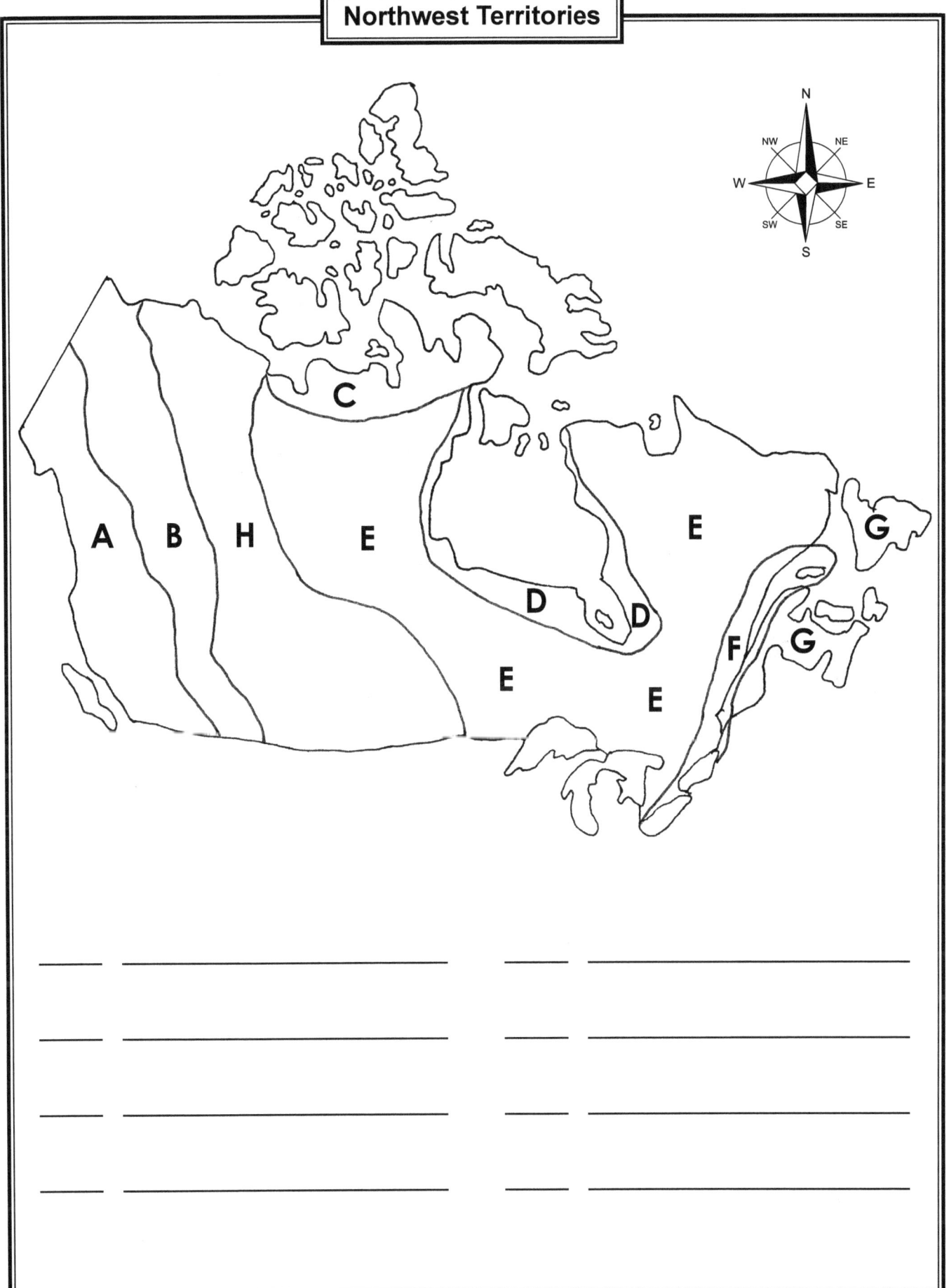

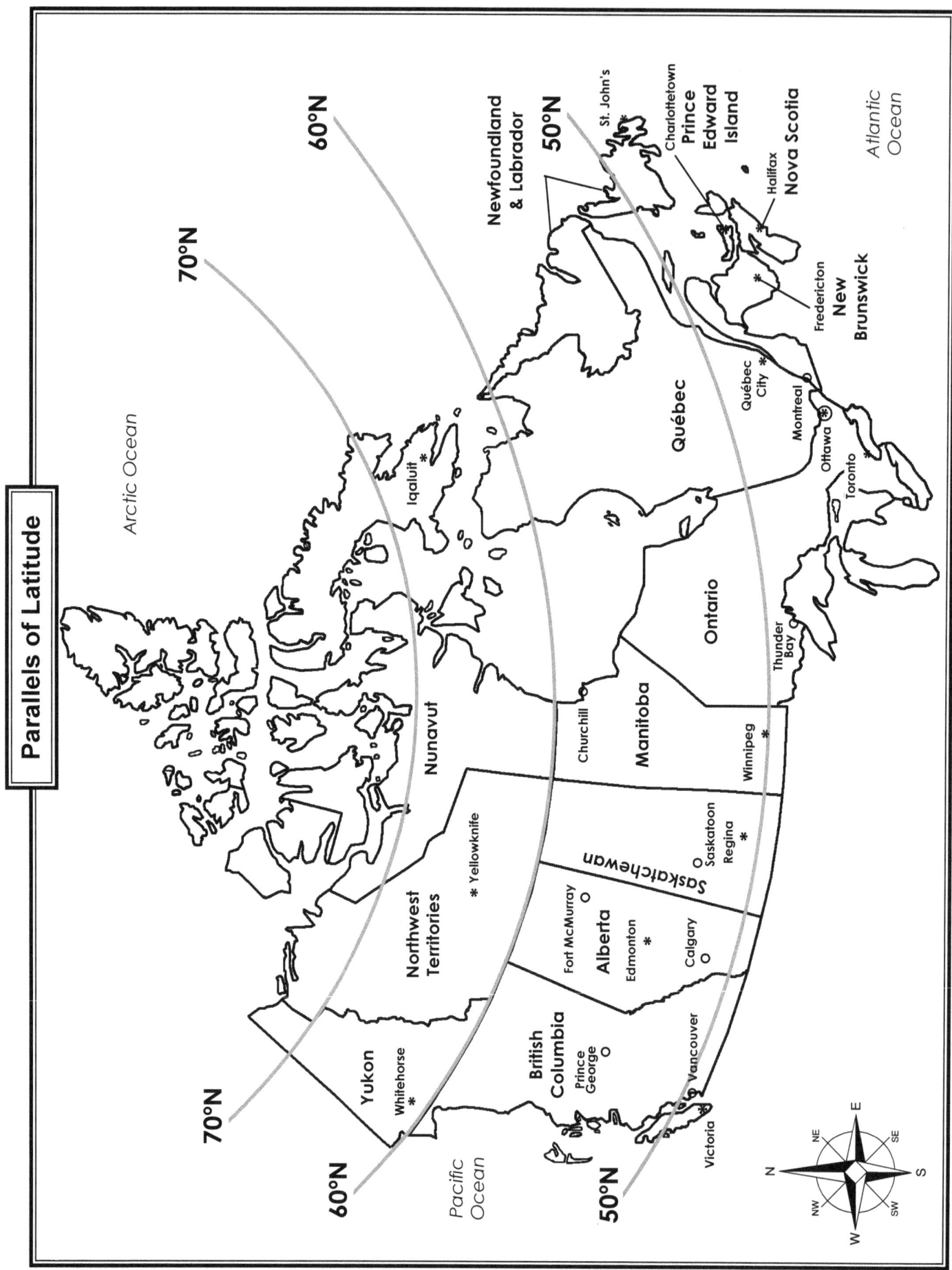

Meridians of Longitude

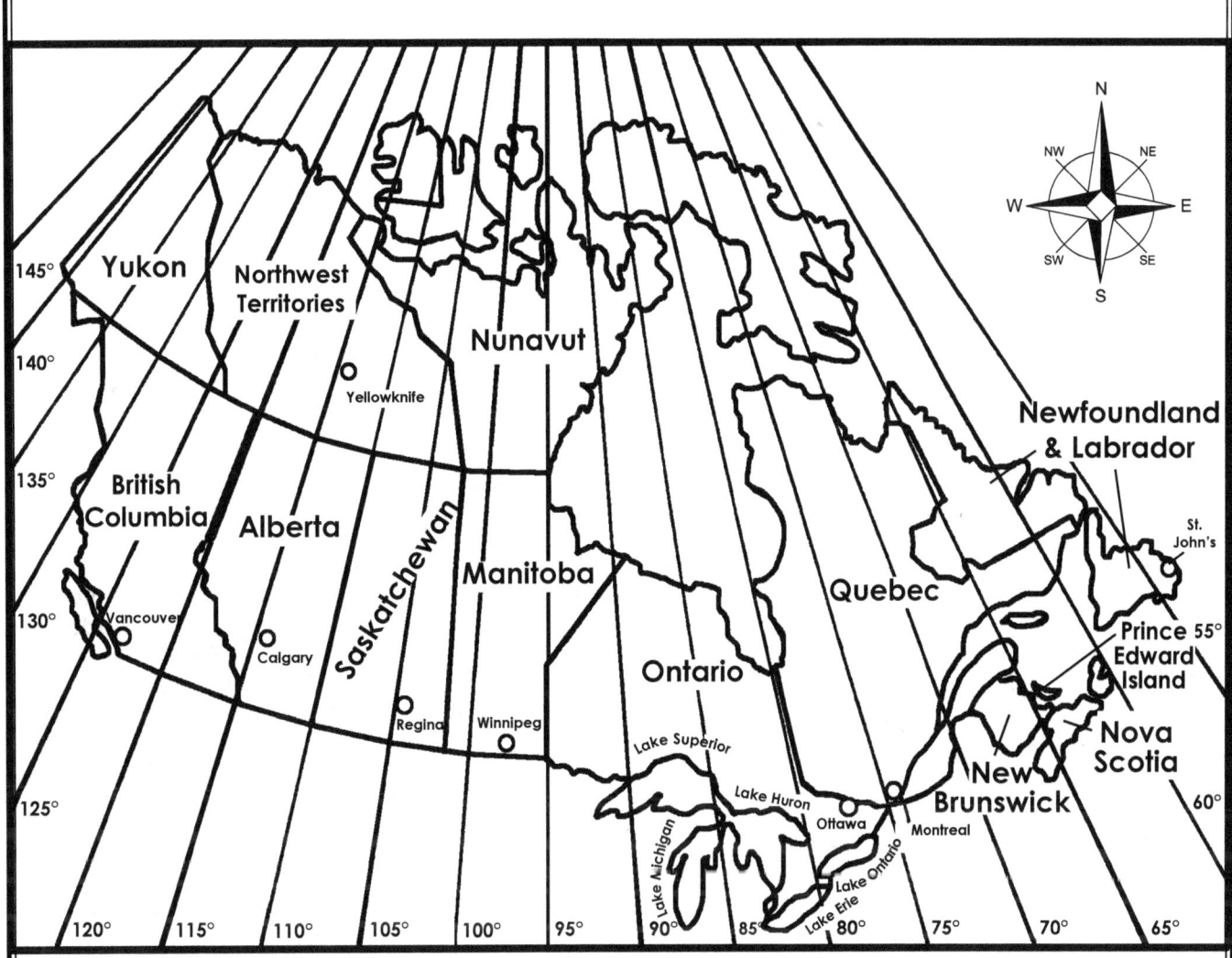

Use the map above to answer these questions.

1. What city is close to the 125° meridian? _____

2. What city is between 95° and 100° meridian? _____

3. The meridian at 75° lies between which two cities?
   _____ and _____

4. Calgary and Yellowknife are closest to which meridian? _____

5. Which city is east of the 55° meridian? _____

6. Regina is found near the _____ meridian.

Simple Scale

How Far Is It?

A map can tell distance when it has a scale.
Use a small paperclip to measure.

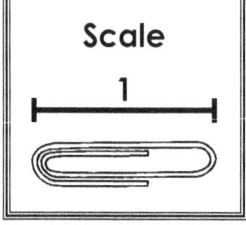

Scale
1

Circle the correct distance:

A to B	3	4	5	6
C to D	2	3	4	5
E to F	3	4	5	6
G to H	2	3	4	5
H to J	1	2	3	4
B to I	1	2	3	4

Simple Scale

A bar scale helps to measure distances on maps.
- Read the bar scale on the map.
- Cut out the bar scale given below the map.
- Use it to measure the following distances.
- Print the distances you measure in the chart.
- Circle the greatest distance.
- Put a rectangle around the smallest distance.

Where You Live	Place in Canada	Distance in km
	Iqaluit, Nunavut	
	Victoria, British Columbia	
	St. John's, Newfoundland and Labrador	
	Ottawa, Ontario	

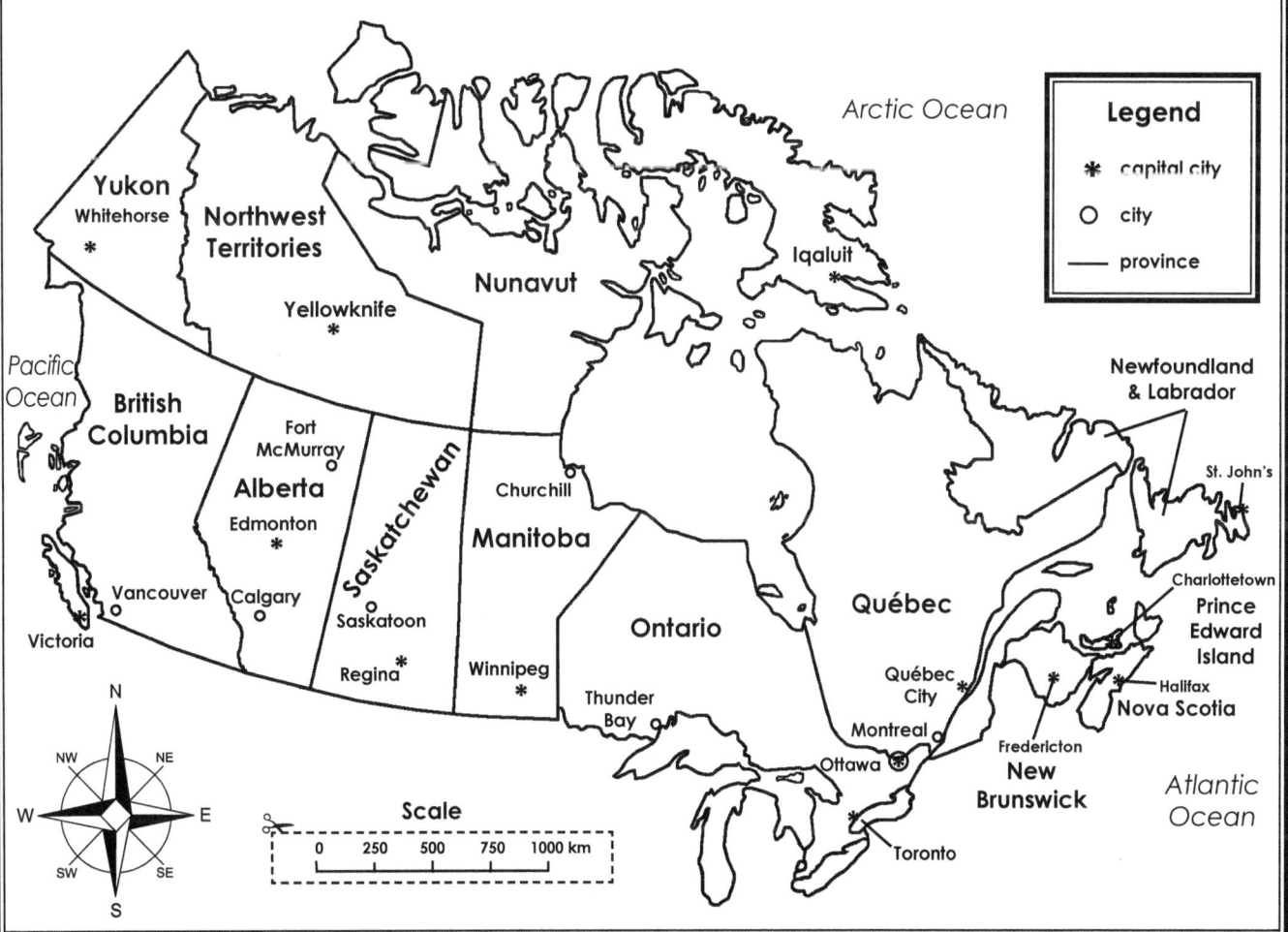

Hemispheres

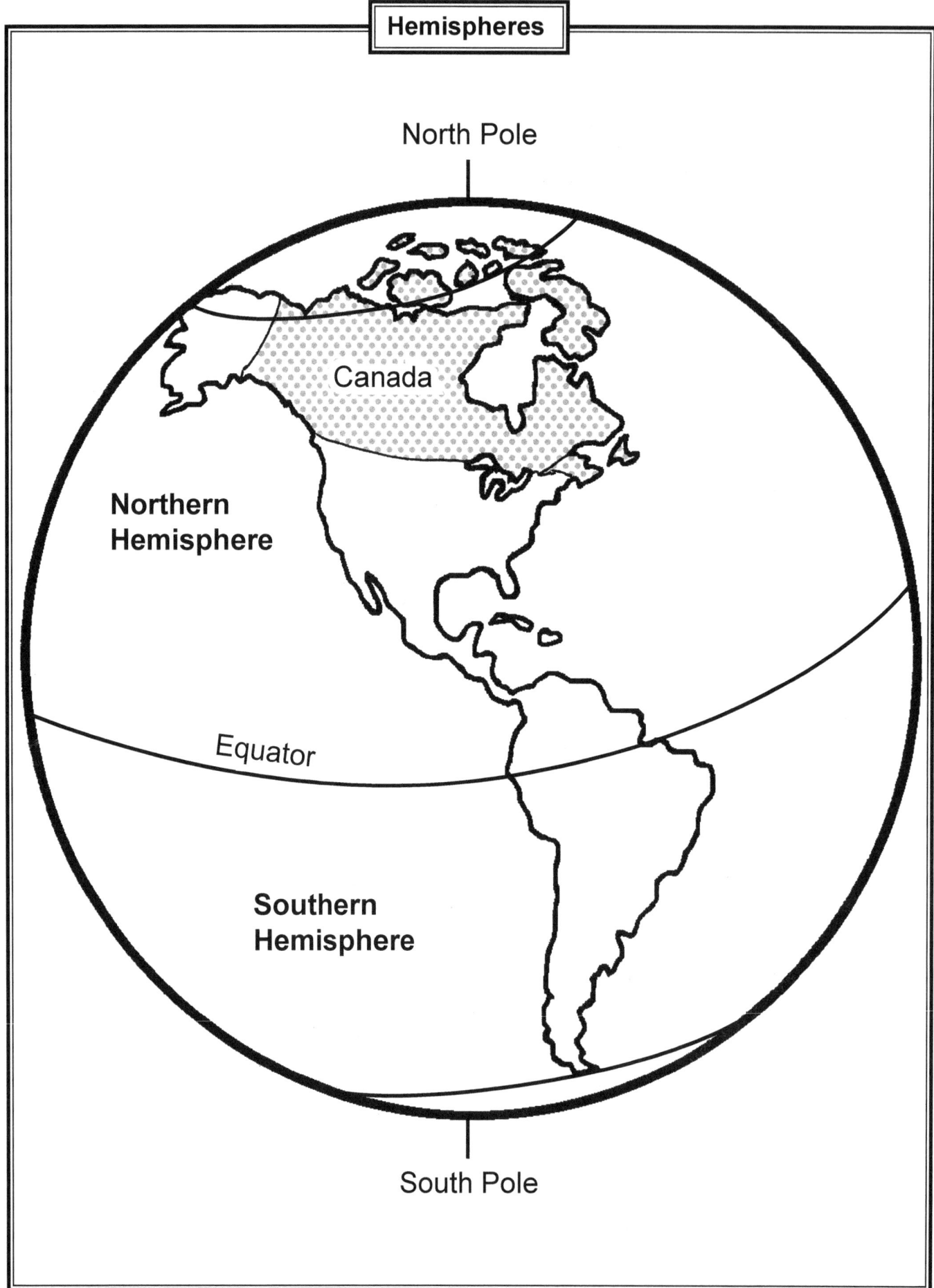

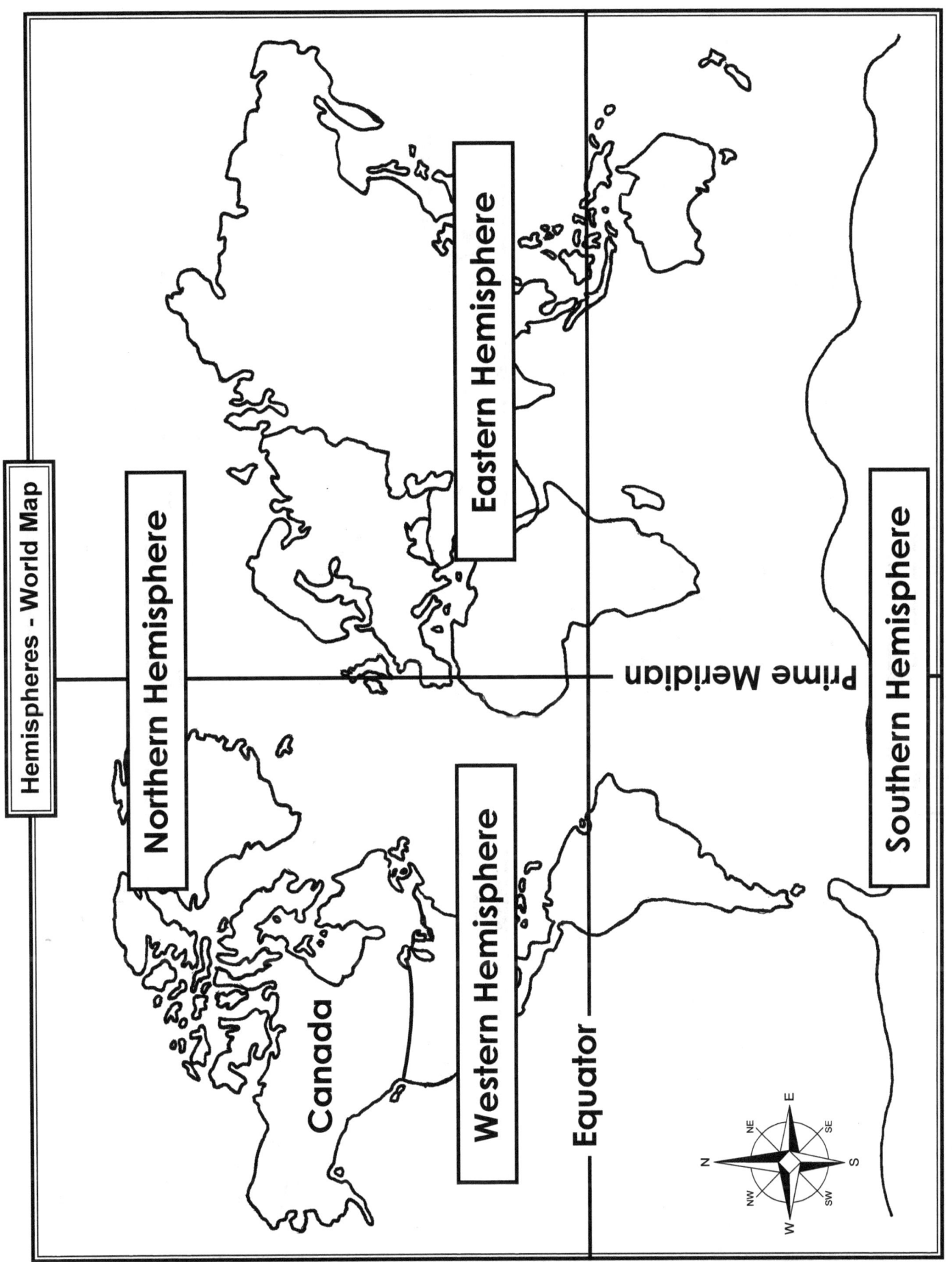

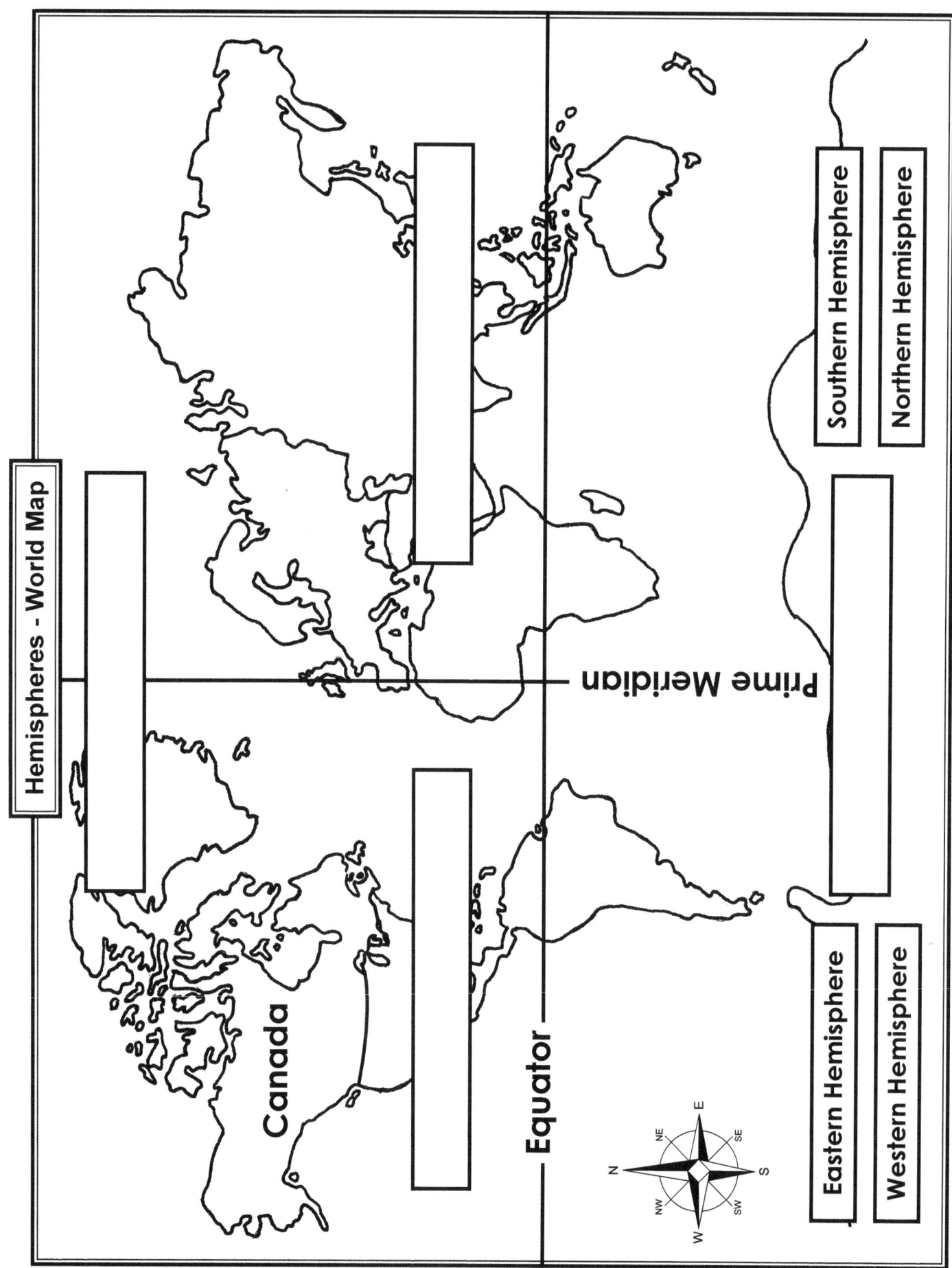

Cardinal Directions

A compass rose tells directions on a map.

Circle **N** in North.   Circle **E** in East.
Circle **S** in South.   Circle **W** in West.

Put **N**, **S**, **W**, and **E** on the compass rose

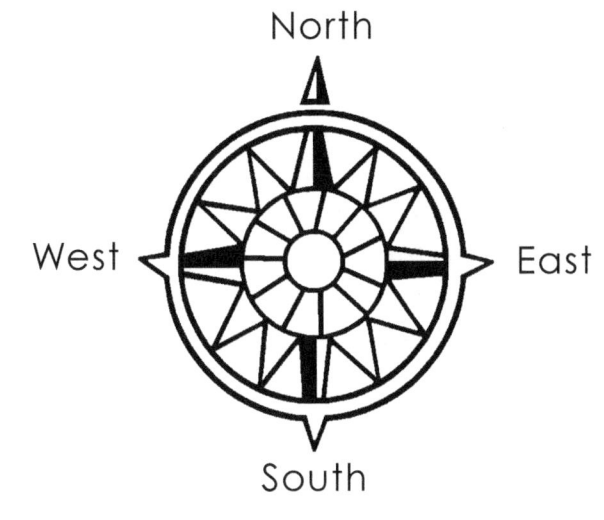

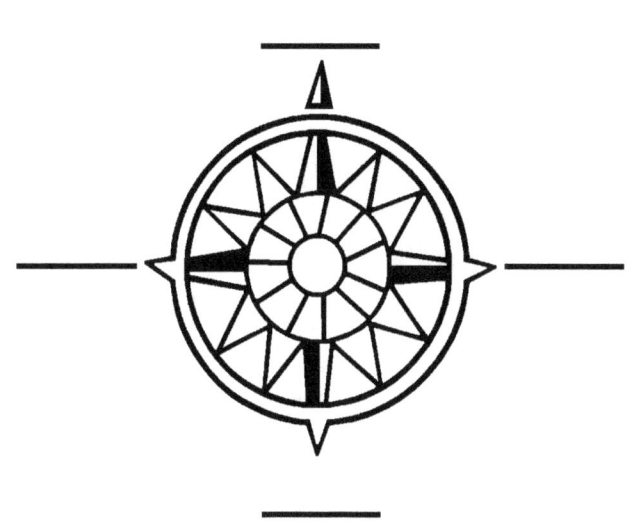

Circle the compass rose on this map of Canada.

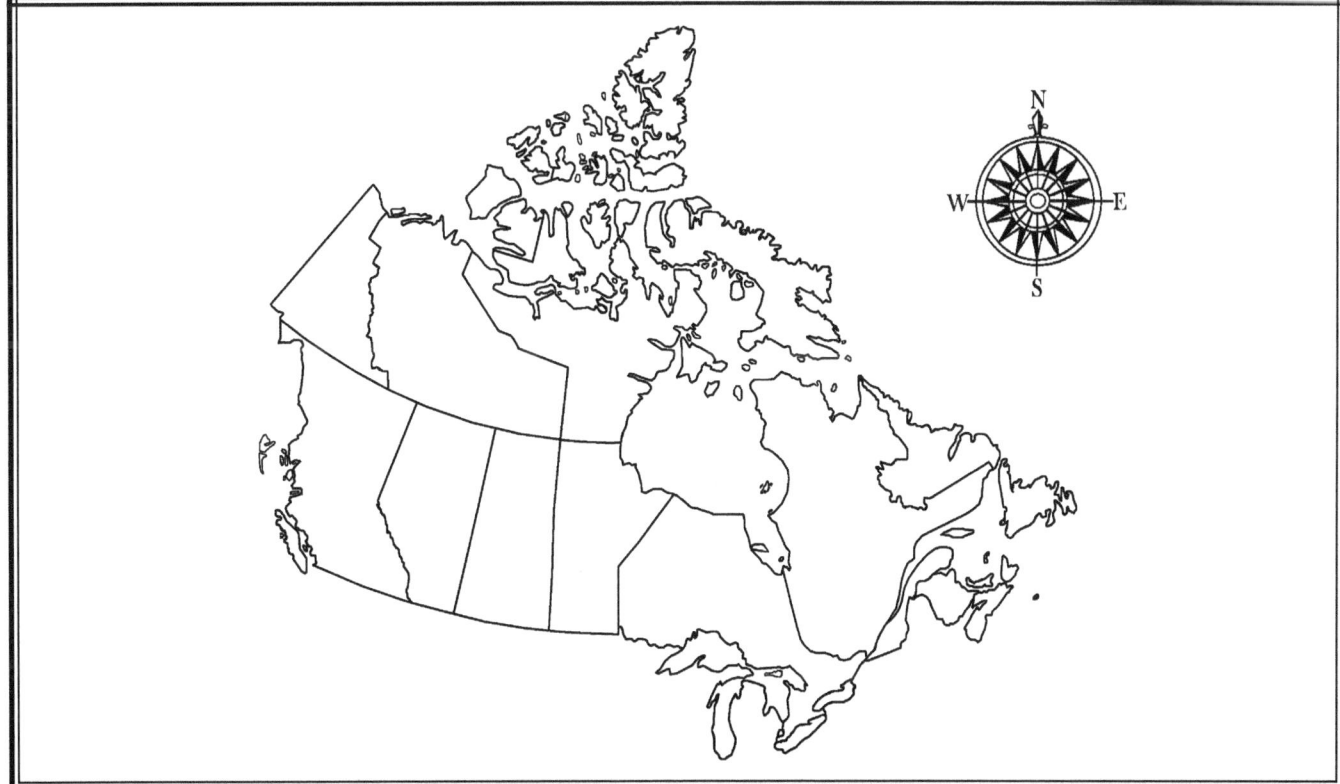

Intermediate Directions

A compass rose tells directions on a map.

Circle the Intermediate Directions (**NE, SE, SW, NW**)	Add **SW, NW, SE** and **NE** to the compass rose.
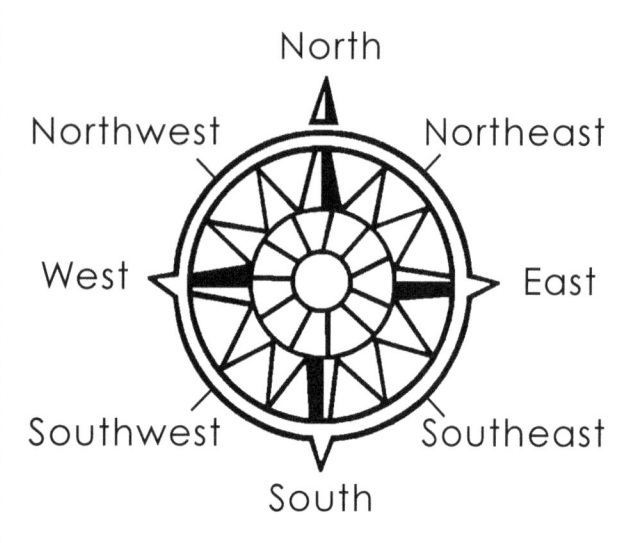	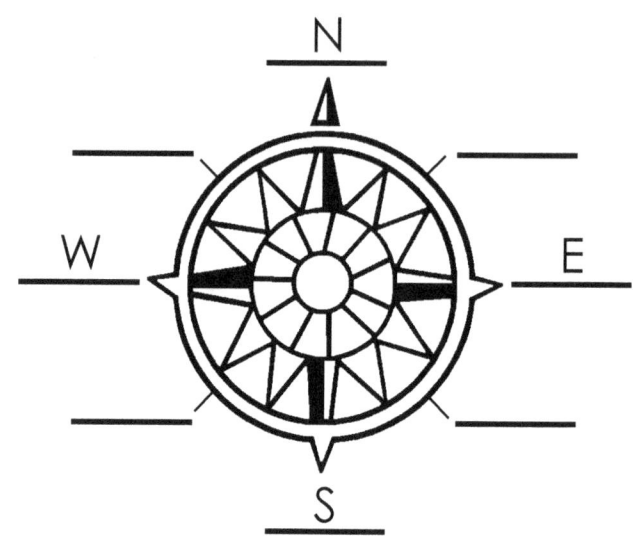

Circle the compass rose on this map of Canada. Add **NE, NW, SE** and **SW** to the compass rose.

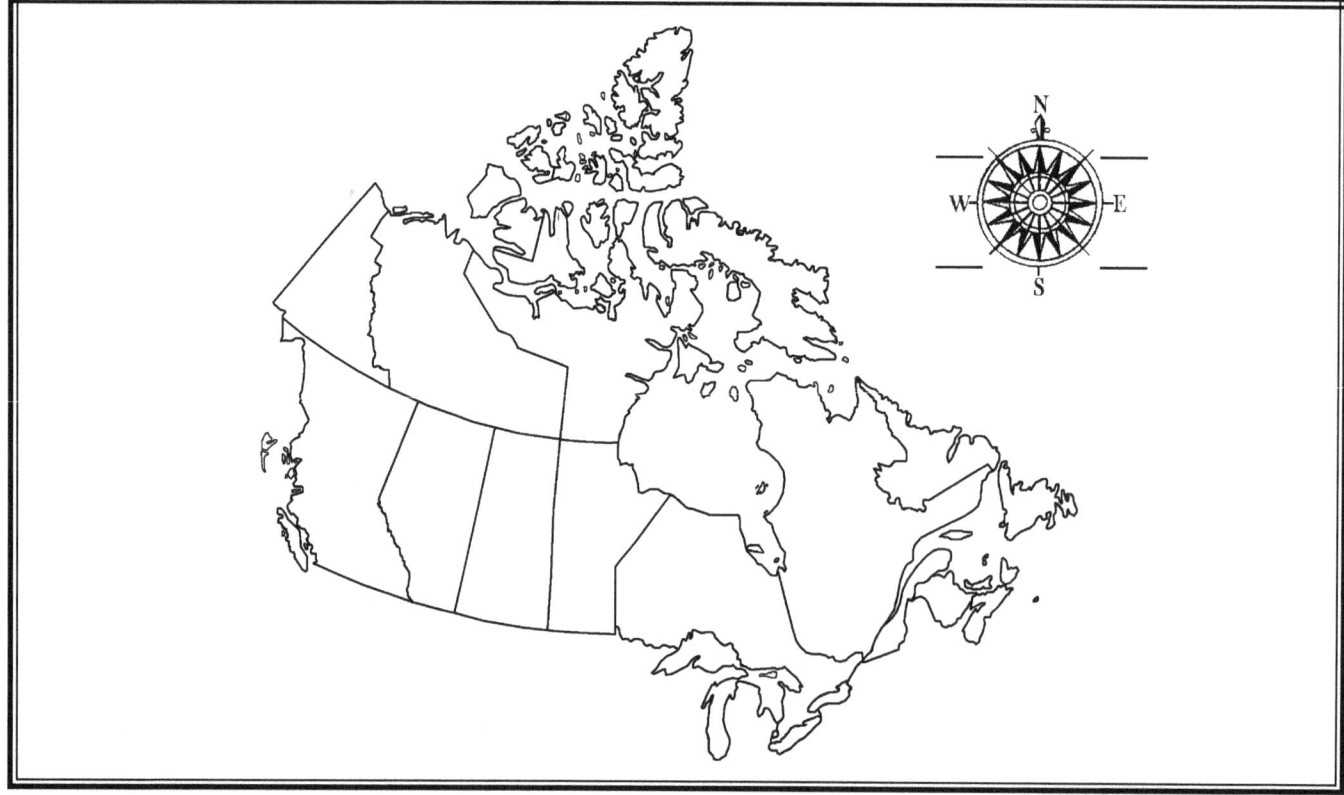

The Great Lakes

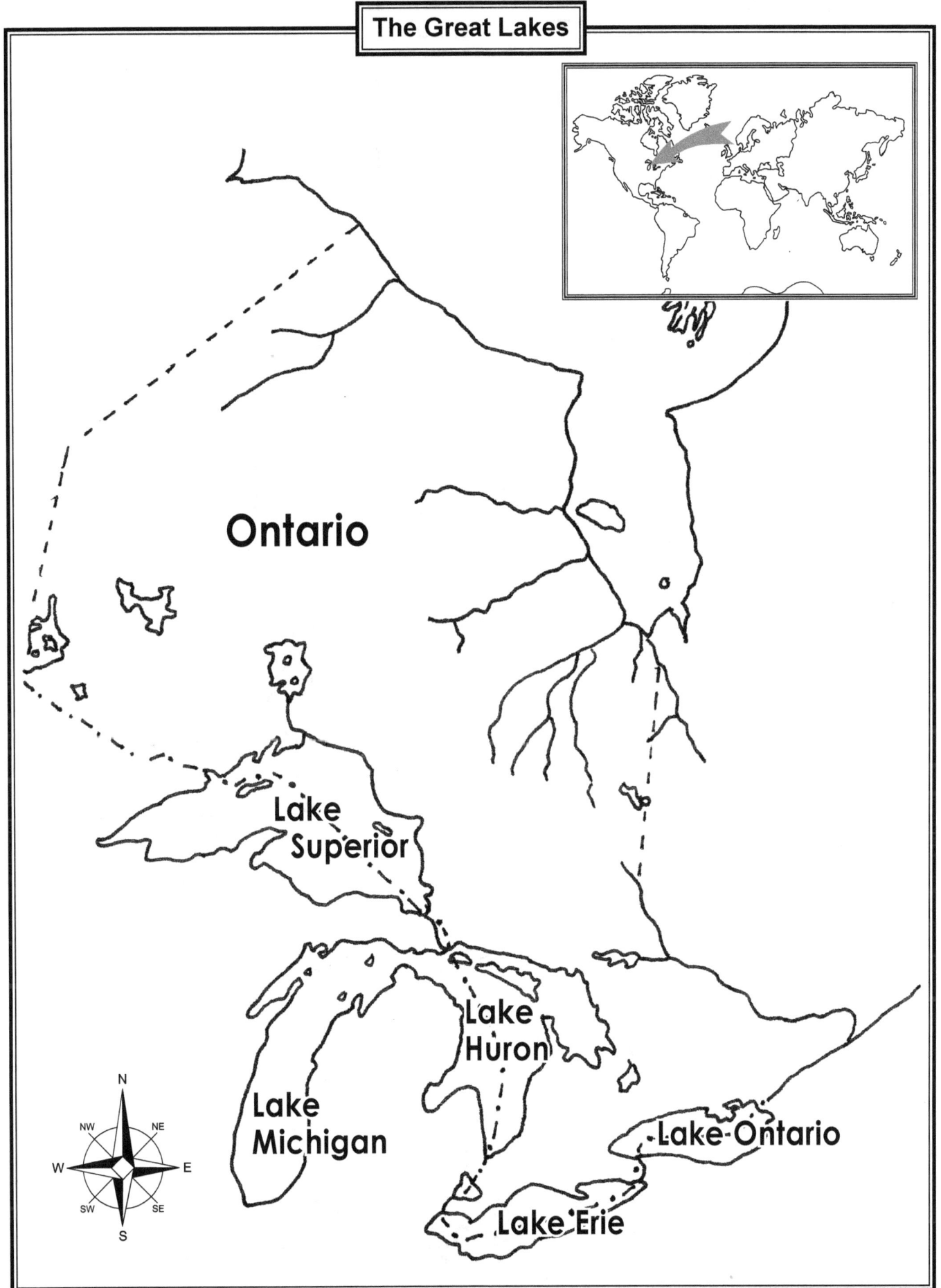

The Great Lakes

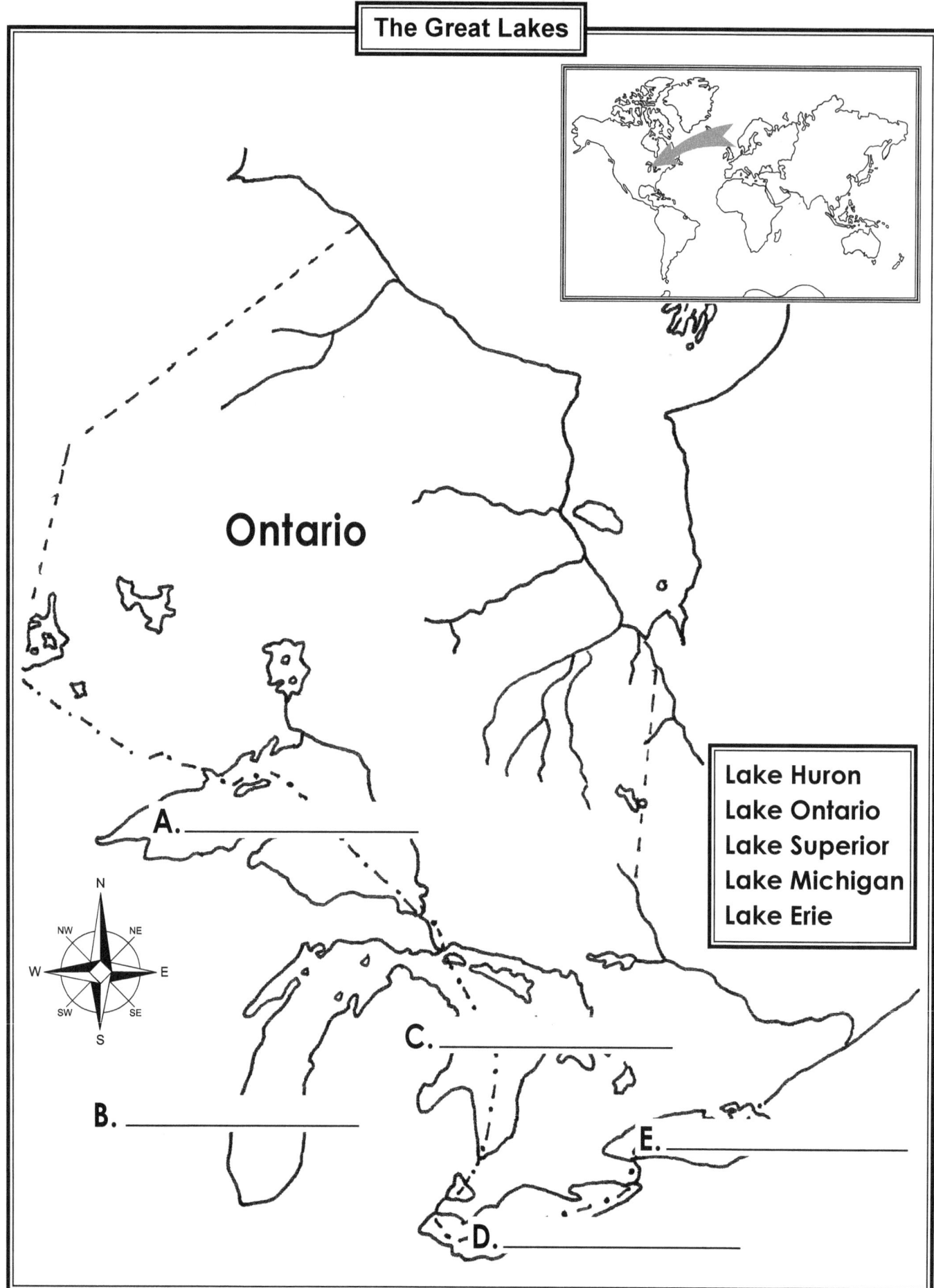

A. _____
B. _____
C. _____
D. _____
E. _____

Lake Huron
Lake Ontario
Lake Superior
Lake Michigan
Lake Erie

Canada's Larger Lakes

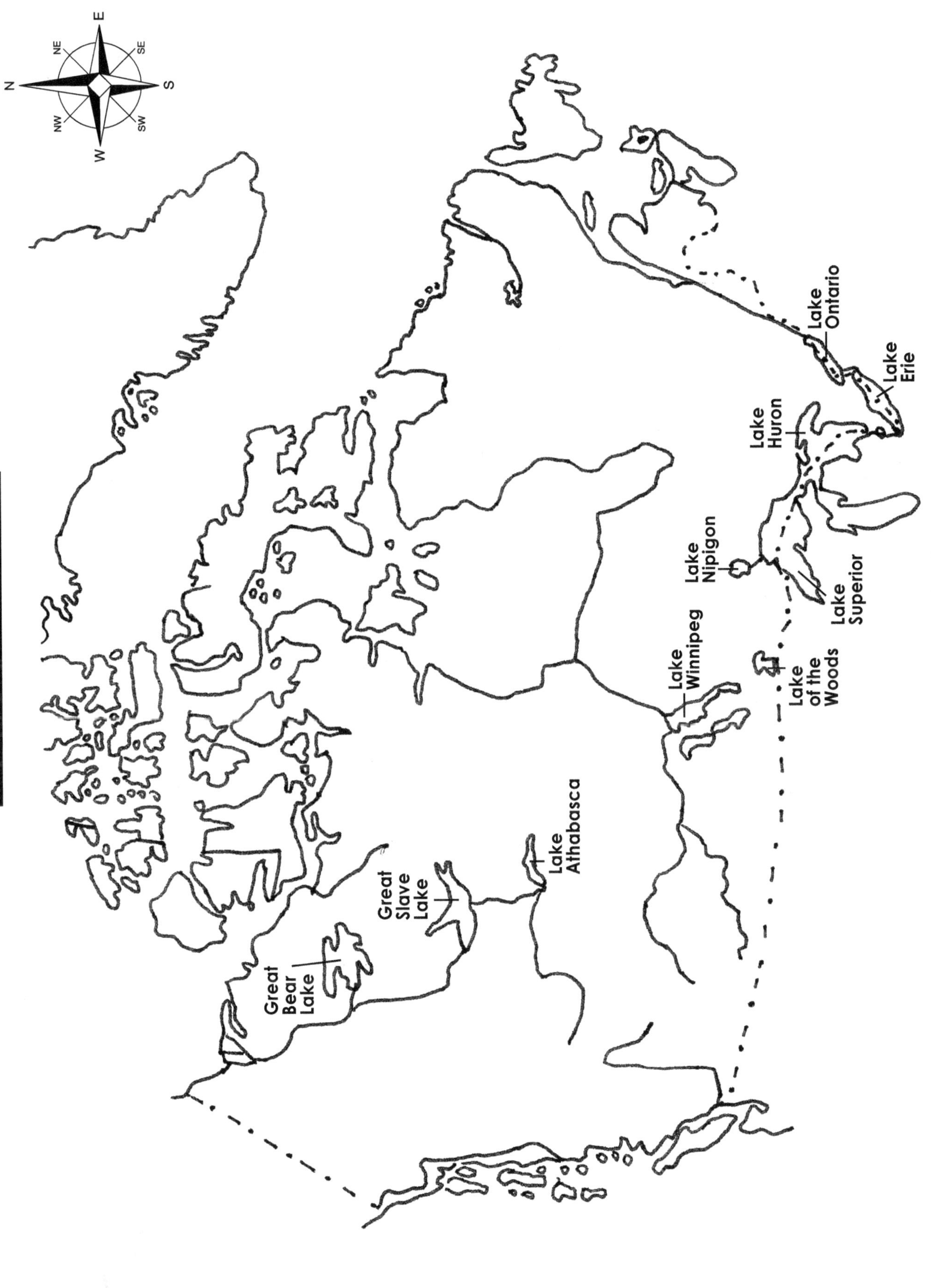

- Lake Ontario
- Lake Erie
- Lake Huron
- Lake Nipigon
- Lake Superior
- Lake Winnipeg
- Lake of the Woods
- Lake Athabasca
- Great Slave Lake
- Great Bear Lake

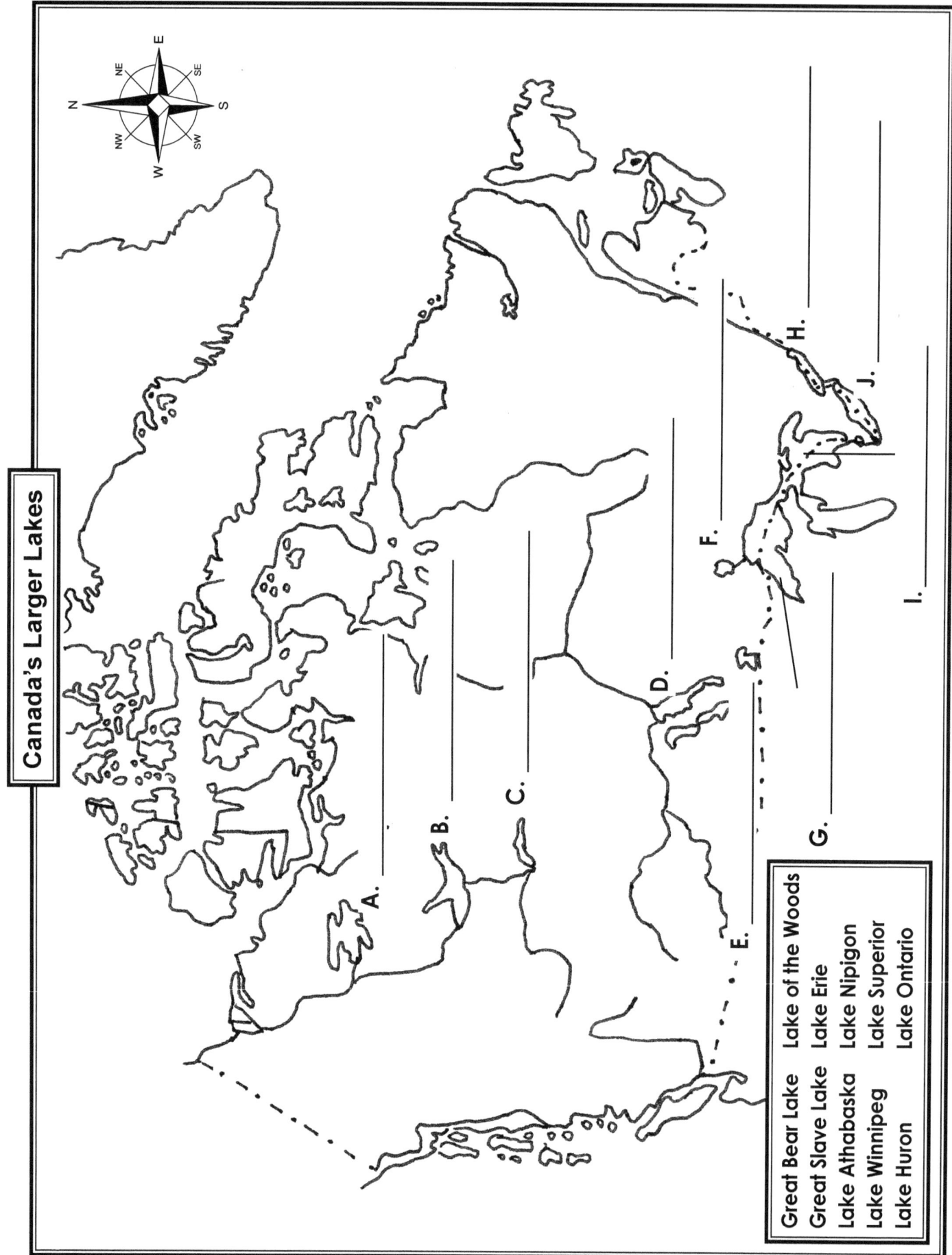

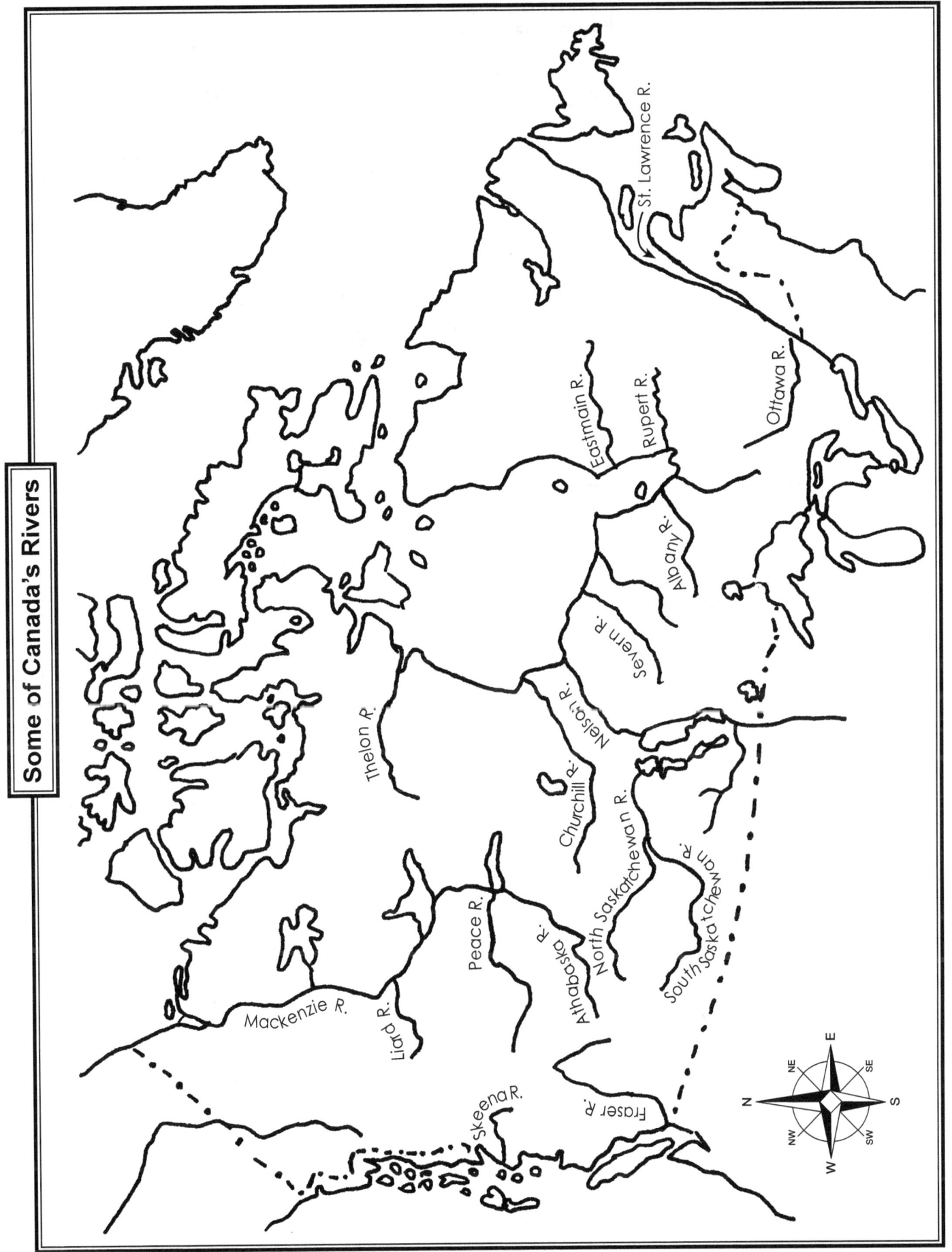

Canada Map Cards

Use these cards for games, activities and assignments.

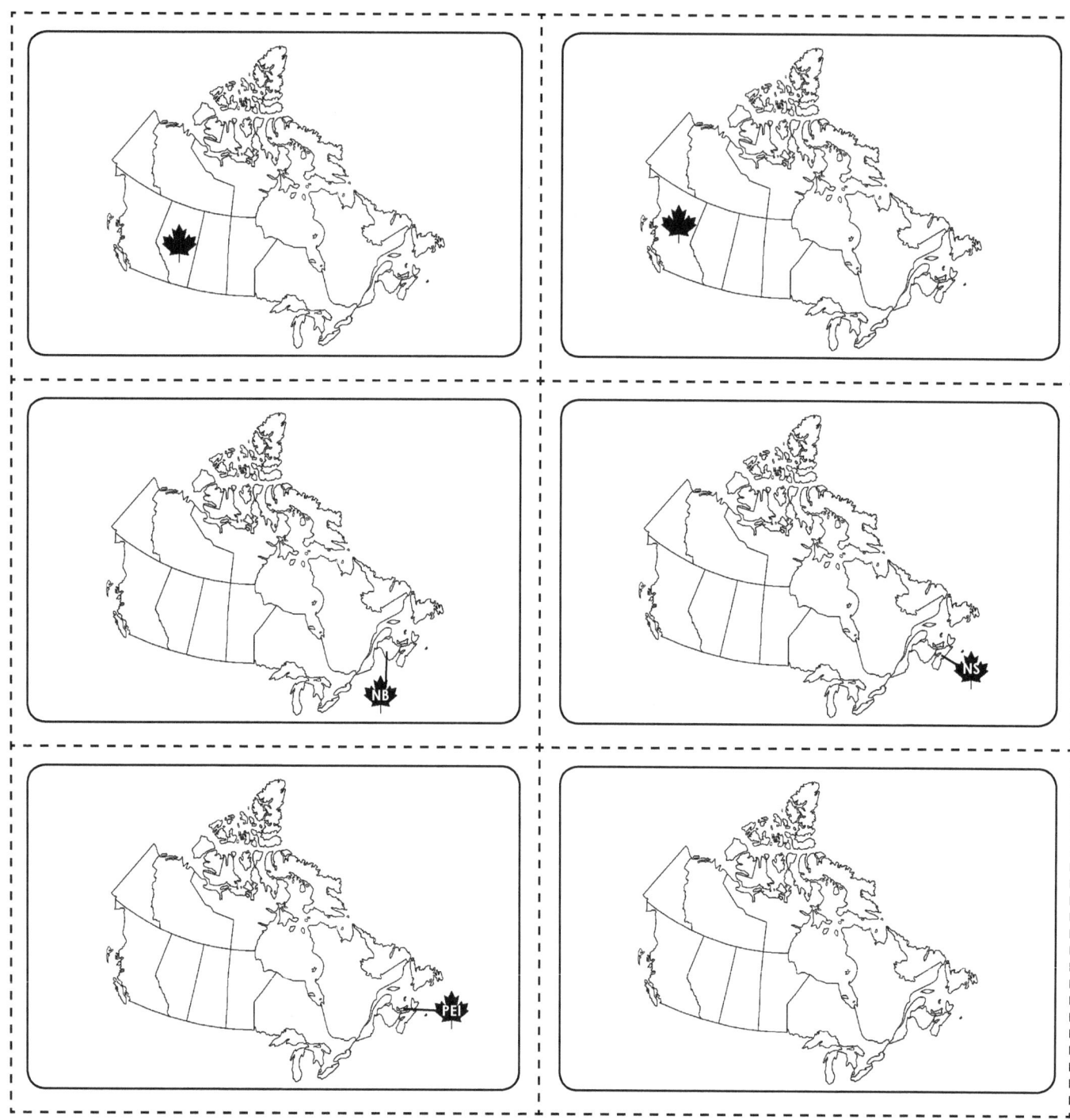

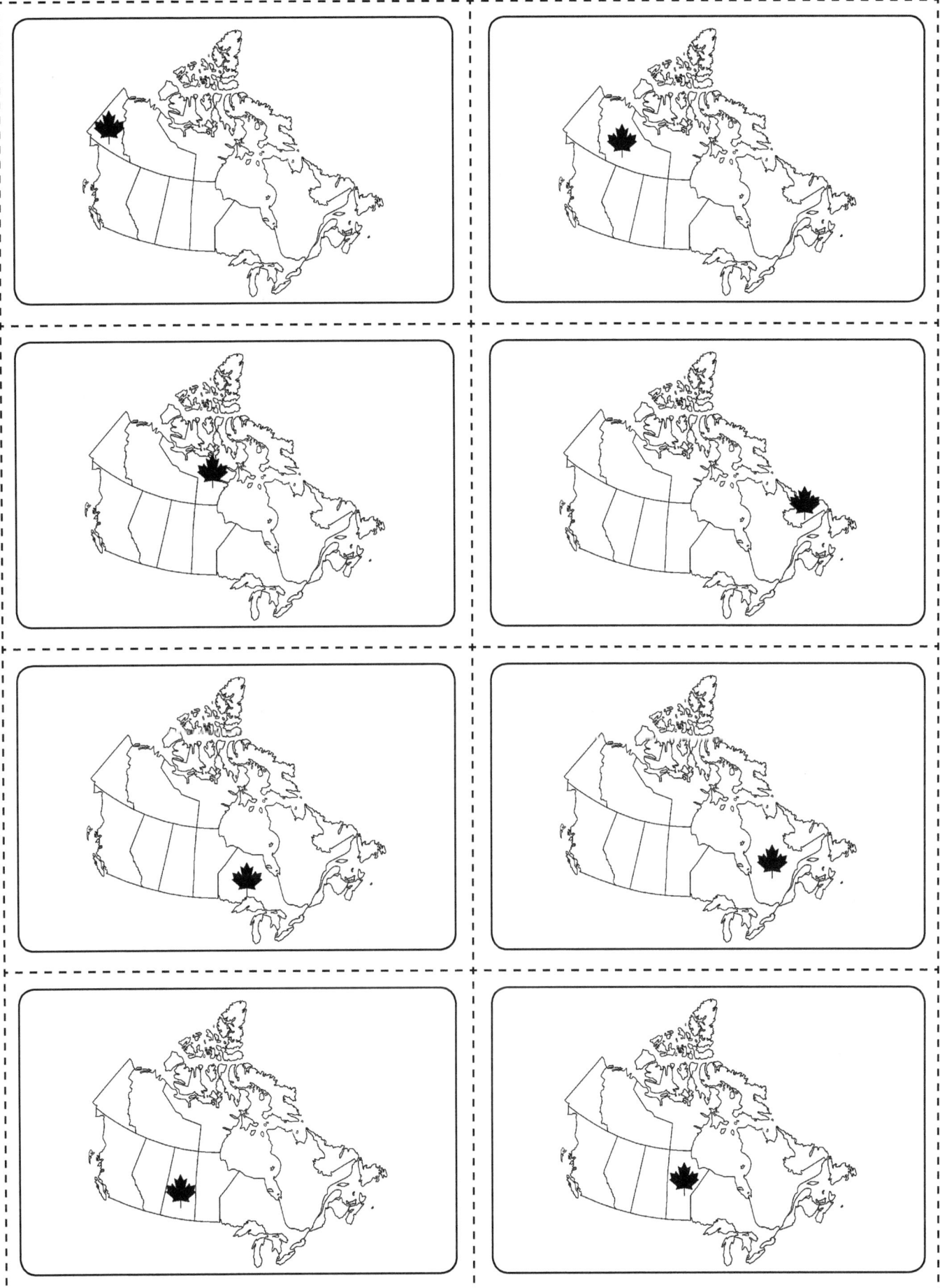

Canada Outline Maps
Answer Key

Canada in the World *Page 6*:
1. North America 2. South America 3. Antarctica 4. Europe 5. Asia 6. Africa
7. Australia

Canada in North America *Page 9*:
1. United States 2. Canada 3. United States 4. Mexico 5. Central America

Canada on a Grid Map *Page 14*:
1. B3 2. D8 3. D2 4. E6 5. E1 6. B6

Canada's Provinces and Territories *Page 16*:
1. Yukon 2. Northwest Territories 3. Nunavut 4. Québec 5. Newfoundland and Labrador 6. British Columbia 7. Alberta 8. Saskatchewan 9. Manitoba 10. Ontario
11. New Brunswick 12. Nova Scotia 13. Prince Edward Island

A. Whitehorse B. Yellowknife C. Iqaluit D. Québec City E. St John's F. Victoria
G. Edmonton H. Regina I. Winnipeg J. Toronto K. Fredericton L. Halifax
M. Charlottetown

Canada's Main Bodies of Water *Page 19*:
1. Beaufort Sea 2. Arctic Ocean 3. Baffin Bay 4. Davis Strait 5. Labrador Sea
6. Atlantic Ocean 7. Gulf of St. Lawrence 8. Atlantic Ocean 9. Lake Ontario
10. Lake Erie 11. Lake Superior 12. Pacific Ocean 13. Hudson Bay 14. James Bay
15. Lake Huron 16. Georgian Bay

Physical Regions *Page 47*:
C. Arctic Lowlands B. Rocky Mountains F. Great Lakes - St Lawrence Lowlands
G. Appalachian H. Interior Plains (Prairies) A. Highlands E. Canadian Shield
D. Hudson Bay Lowlands

Meridians of Longitude *Page 49*:
1. Vancouver 2. Winnipeg 3. Ottawa and Montreal 4. 115 degrees 5. St John's
6. 105 degrees

Simple Scale *Page 50*:
A to **B** 4; **C** to **D** 3; **E** to **F** 4; **G** to **H** 3; **H** to **J** 3; **B** to **I** 1

The Great Lakes *Page 58*:
A. Lake Superior B. Lake Michigan C. Lake Huron D. Lake Erie E. Lake Ontario

Canada's Larger Lakes *Page 60*:
A. Great Bear Lake B. Great Slave Lake C. Lake Athabasca D. Lake Winnipeg
E. Lake of the Woods F. Lake Nipigon G. Lake Superior H. Lake Ontario I. Lake Huron
J. Lake Erie

www.ingramcontent.com/pod-product-compliance
Lightning Source LLC
Chambersburg PA
CBHW062133160426
43191CB00013B/2286